MW00814867

Developing
Strategic
Partnerships

Developing Strategic Partnerships

How to leverage more business from major customers

Chris Steward

Gower

© Chris Steward 1999

All rights reserved. No part of this publication may be reproduced, stored in a retrieval system, or transmitted in any form or by any means, electronic, mechanical, photocopying, recording or otherwise without the permission of the publisher.

Published by
Gower Publishing Limited
Gower House
Croft Road
Aldershot
Hampshire GU11 3HR
England

Gower
Old Post Road
Brookfield
Vermont 05025
USA

Chris Steward has asserted his right under the Copyright, Designs and Patents Act 1988 to be identified as the author of this work.

British Library Cataloguing in Publication Data
Steward, Chris
    Developing strategic partnerships : how to leverage more
    business from major customers
    1. Strategic alliances (Business) 2.Business networks
    I.Title
    658'.044

    ISBN 0 566 08101 6

Typeset by SetPoint, Middlesex and printed in the United Kingdom at the University Press, Cambridge

Contents

Figures

Tables

Introduction

The benefits of customer alliances

This book is aimed at the business practitioner. It is a 'how to' text that in addition embodies the theoretical elements necessary for a proper understanding of the subject. Reading it should enable the practitioner to design a strategic partnership plan and execute initiatives with selected customers and suppliers. 'Strategic', since partnerships are very powerful tools in ensuring continuing, profitable supply at either end of the value chain and, as such, are an integral part of a firm's strategy. 'Selected', because strategic partnerships are not for every customer or supplier. As we shall see, the resources and commitment vital to ensure success dictate that only a handful of partnership initiatives can be tackled at any one time, even by the wealthiest of firms. Many partnerships can be entered into over time by the majority of firms, but it is a question of phasing and applying resources to the best available opportunities.

A strategic partnership can exist simultaneously between a firm and its suppliers, and between it and its customers. Among the principal benefits arising from partnerships fulfilling the necessary criteria are the following:

- Ensuring continuity of supply in markets where the supply side dominates, or where supplies are liable to seasonal or some other volatility or can be subject to interruption from time to time.
- Less competitive friction with suppliers, who understand more about the firm they are supplying and its specific product and service needs. The same principle applies when considering the relationship between the firm and its customers.
- Raising exit barriers to customers and suppliers who might be tempted to switch. A strategic partnership does not make this impossible, just more difficult.
- Raising competitive entry barriers, making it harder for competitors to gain entry to the firm's customer or supplier base. As we shall see, there is no room for two strategic partners in the same product-market with the same customer or supplier. Therefore, strategic partnerships also have first-mover advantages.
- Lowering entry barriers for the introduction of new products and services, and for change in general, to suppliers and customers with whom a partnership has been built.

■ Lower transaction costs, because partnerships that are properly constructed reduce, or in some cases eliminate, costly transactions between firms.

■ More opportunity for profit making, since it is more probable that two partners working closely together can create synergistic energy that can be directed into profit-building actions. These actions then become jointly undertaken rather than one party suggesting and proposing to the other in a normal buyer–seller relationship.

■ Greater stability of profit, because the future is more certain inside a strategic partnership than outside it.

There is a blueprint for building a strategic partnership, illustrated as Figure 3.2. Following this modular layout, the material in this book is divided into three parts.

Part I – Making strategy choices

In the first part we will examine some theoretical concepts concerning both generic and marketing strategies that are open to most firms in most circumstances, developing some ideas on how to select the most appropriate one. In Chapter 1, Degrees of Freedom, the three broad strategy choices facing firms will be explored, together with an analysis of the forces which limit a firm's freedom to act. Chapter 2, Real Competitive Differential, contains theoretical ideas about the nature of commercial advantage and, importantly, adds the practical dimension of how to translate this into action. The strategic partnership model is examined in detail in Chapter 3, and it is here that the distinction between the various types of business partnership will be explained.

Part II – Planning for a strategic alliance

The chapters comprising Part II deal with the internal planning aspects of partnership strategy, up to the point where the initiative goes 'live', the prospective partner is contacted and a proposal made. Chapter 4 discusses why and how internal approval for a partnership must be gained. In Chapter 5, we can see the process for profiling and selecting potential partners. Finally, the concept and practice of strategic partnership initiatives as the basis for a successful alliance will be detailed in Chapter 6.

Part III – Implementing and sustaining an alliance

The material in Part III covers the steps between making the first customer or supplier contact and putting the partnership in place. It begins with a step-by-step look at gaining customer commitment in Chapter 7. The technical and commercial study, its evaluation and the second customer presentation are all addressed in Chapter 8. Chapter 9, The SPI Team Approach, explains how the team should be selected and led and how the work can be scoped and scheduled. Evaluating strategic partnerships is the subject of Chapter 10, and the final chapter addresses the vital matter of how to sustain an alliance, sometimes in the face of adversity.

Why strategic partnerships are necessary

As mature and maturing markets polarize, there is a strong tendency for a small number of firms to end up controlling distribution channels. Examples of this can be found virtually everywhere. Markets tend to polarize as they mature, for example between firms offering a 'no frills' approach and those offering a premium benefits package. It is the choice between Lada and BMW. Simultaneously, and as shake-out occurs, a few firms grab the lion's share of trade at each polarity point, resulting in these firms controlling distribution channels. The US government has alleged that Microsoft is abusing its dominant position by controlling access to the Internet through its browser. Major UK food retailers received some bad press in recent months concerning their role in the decline of the corner shop and of town centre shopping. This inevitably means that suppliers to these markets face a situation where a handful of immensely powerful customers represent a large, and probably grow-ing, share of their sales and profits. Firms facing this situation have developed many different strategies to address this imbalance – some successful, others less so.

This book describes one potential path to sustainable profitability: strategic partnerships. However, the road to partnership nirvana is strewn with casualties, caused mainly because an imperfect understand-ing of the term exists, or because one side has in mind an unequal part-nership. It is in this sense that some businesspeople have abused the word 'partnership', with unfortunate, and sometimes lasting, conse-quences for those involved. The aim of this book is to show how true partnerships can be defined, potential partners identified and long-lasting and profitable relationships built.

If the competitive climate is already severe for most firms, the strong likelihood is that it will become more rather than less so over time. This has important strategic implications, not least of which is the role that business partnerships will play as the future unfolds. As already suggested, strategic partnerships with key suppliers can help ensure secure supplies and those with major customers can help deliver stable profitability.

Firms that see a strategic partnership as a means of securing supply, satisfying customers and making sustainable profit should begin taking action now that will become even more necessary as competition intensifies. 'Prediction,' said Niels Bohr, pioneer of the work that led to the atomic bomb, 'is very difficult, especially about the future.' Foresight has always been a real practical difficulty. The best we can hope for is to obtain glimpses of the future from time to time. And any reasonably accurate insight into the future, however imperfect, will be of some help in planning today what must be done tomorrow.

A changing competitive climate

We can glimpse some aspects of the relatively near future by studying trends and statistical data, and by the use of forecasting tools such as econometric modelling. It is a cliché that the future starts here, but the relevance of forecasting to the material in this book is that partnerships are intended to be long lasting. Partnerships begun today should have a life of many years and, ideally, be conceived as a strategy spanning a decade or more. One of the few statements concerning the future that can be made with a degree of certainty is that the future informs the present just as much as the other way round. Knowledge of how the near future can be managed to commercial advantage will be of interest to most business practitioners, and it is in this context that the following forecast applies to strategic partnerships.

The nature of competition will change in several ways over the next decade or two and will be driven by four main factors: information access, consumerism, emerging markets and global alliances. There are a number of future and current scenarios in which these factors cross-fertilize and feed off one another.

Information access

A few years ago, the notion that the majority of advertisers would quote their World Wide Web address at the bottom of the TV screen would have been laughable. Internet experts claim that we are at the dawn of a global information access revolution. The Internet will speed up the adoption of English as the world's predominant language for business generally and information specifically. A single telephone number, on which a subscriber can be reached anywhere in the world, is just around the corner. Videoconferencing, a relatively new communication medium, will soon be superseded by combined picture/sound transmission facilities.

Speed of product adoption is becoming faster and faster. It is no longer the exclusive domain of the international business community to be the first to have access to new technology. Schoolchildren are among the first users of handheld electronic technology in the form of games, and that speeds the learning curve so that, in later life, they quickly adopt handheld technology when it is introduced in the domestic and business arenas. New technology seems likely to continue to drive information access forward. 'On the go' communications technology, artificial intelligence systems, 'smart' materials able to change structure to interact better with the environment, increasing advances in miniaturization – these are not science fiction, but technology fact. The real point about this new technology is that access to it is almost universal. We are moving swiftly towards a world that has been described as consisting of 'seamless networks of data, voice and moving pictures'.

The challenge for individuals as well as firms is to learn to manage these 'seamless networks' and to use them to search for fresh sources of competitive advantage. Whole new industries are emerging and within them many new firms will spring up. Some existing organizations will wither, others will grow and some will form alliances. Either way, the intensity of competition and speed of adoption factors combined will widen the gap between the best and the rest.

Emerging markets

According to the United Nations, there will be between 8 and 9 billion people on the planet by the year 2025, an increase over 1996 of approximately 2 to 3 billion. Most of this growth will take place in developing countries. The USA, Japanese and most western European populations will 'grey', with the percentage of those over 60 years old increasing. The same scenario is also likely in China and Latin America. At the same time, the world's population is getting younger. By the beginning of the twenty-first century, it is estimated that half the global population will be under the age of 20.

A number of East Asian countries, parts of Latin America and India and several eastern European countries will have burgeoning economies by 2010. Taking them as a group for the purpose of economic evaluation, the World Bank reported in its 1996 statistics that these countries will account for some 20 per cent of global GDP by 2010, double their present figure. China may have overtaken the USA as the world's biggest economy by the same date and could have a commanding lead 10 years later. Precisely what this means for business, products and services, those that exist and those yet to be developed, depends on the industry in which a firm is situated, but the effects will be profound, not least in the realm of strategic partnerships.

Consumerism

It is not only in the countries and regions mentioned above where consumerism will make its power felt – the top 20 per cent of western consumers will experience a real rise in living standards. These future outcomes seem likely to be accompanied by a continuing widening of the gap between rich and poor. At the same time, more and more people are already feeling alienated by what they perceive as the 'distant control' of government, science and the ever increasing pace and complexity of life. Signs are evident in the USA and elsewhere in western society of a search for some kind of group identity. This manifests itself in the adoption of Asian value systems, 'new age' religions and even designer brands.

In the new competitive paradigm, 'virtual communities' will exist, centred on the home or office. They will enable firms to create virtual alliances and give individuals the ability to personalize their space. Internet and TV shopping, as well as more traditional distribution channels, will offer consumers a bewildering array of products, services and, equally important, shopping experiences. New channel distributors will combine with manufacturers and others to open up important fresh opportunities.

One of the effects of changing values will be that fewer qualified people will want to work in what they increasingly see as torpid, systemized organizations. Instead, a growing number of highly qualified people in both developed and transitional market economies will choose employment that only recently would have seemed precarious. They will work for several employers at once and will become highly prized. The ability of firms to capture and retain these people will depend not only on the financial benefits, but also on the quality and challenge of the work offered. There are many ways in which work can be enriched, made more rewarding in the fullest sense, and partnerships between firms are one of these.

Global alliances

Global alliances already exist. They are one result of liberalized capital flows in the world's economies. Financial markets will become even more powerful during the next two decades, often weakening the ability of governments to act. We have already seen governments' inability to counter speculative currency attacks in several celebrated cases, such as in Thailand in 1997.

Alongside more freedom in capital markets, we can see liberalized world trade. The two co-exist, usually happily. World trade grows with capital, as always, flowing to the best potential returns, but also as a direct result of inter-governmental agreements such as GATT (General Agreement on Tariffs and Trade). Alongside action by governments, giant corporations straddle the globe, owing little allegiance to anyone except shareholders and lenders or investors of capital. They are able to hold national governments to ransom, offering the promise of job creation if grants or other concessions are forthcoming, against the threat of job losses if not. Occurrences of this phenomenon will increase sharply during the next 20 years, creating new alliances between governments and multinational corporations.

Virtual alliances are a distinct possibility during the coming generation. Market size may no longer be a more or less guaranteed source of strength; indeed, small, entrepreneurial firms will be able to use electronic channels on a national, regional or global basis. There will be opportunities for firms, irrespective of size, to form alliances that exist only in virtual reality, but that deliver real benefits to their members. In addition, large firms will gain many benefits from forming partnerships with smaller, innovative organizations.

Of course, it would be foolish to suggest that statistical interpretation and trend analysis, however well conducted, can paint a precise picture of the future. Disturbances and discontinuities are bound to occur. Some of these can be foreseen, often dimly in the shadows, others cannot. The consequences of some will prove to be manageable, others less so. The effects will not be felt to the same degree in every country, in every industry or in every firm. Yet it is the ability of managers to predict and respond positively to shocks that will make the difference. Some things never change.

Then and now

If these are some of the possibilities for the first 20 years of the twenty-first century, the question now facing managers is: what steps should be taken to get ready? The answer, of course, is many things, one of which is the focus of this book. On a wider scale, however, here is a suggested list of 10 items on which managers would do well to concentrate some thinking as they contemplate the future, and the actions needed to manage it.

1   Scanning the horizons – there are several – for areas offering opportunities or posing threats to existing or planned new products, services and businesses. Setting up the systems to achieve this quickly and at low cost.
2   Redefining the goals of the firm and turning these into stretching but attainable objectives.
3   Creating clear strategies for the achievement of business goals and objectives at all levels.
4   Basing goals, objectives and strategies on a deep understanding of organizational capabilities, and having plans to develop core competencies.
5   Understanding the macro chain in which the firm operates and how value is added.
6   Monitoring new technologies and processes and searching for ways to utilize them in the business.
7   Understanding end-user or consumer needs and values, being able to adapt and respond quickly.
8   Designing new work structures that better utilize creative, self-adaptive systems and providing the necessary training.
9   Encouraging innovation among everyone in the workforce.
10 Building strategic partnerships with suppliers and customers for mutual profit and competitive advantage.

Success is not compulsory in any organization and, as with virtually everything else, there is a choice. Broadly, firms can continue as at present, or they can adopt whichever of the new techniques, methodologies, technologies or ideas seem best to fit their particular needs and capabilities, fusing them into the necessary new working practices. This is how most organizations learn – and it seems an eminently sensible way to proceed.

Part I
Making Strategy Choices

Degrees of freedom

To begin setting the context for strategic partnerships, we will first examine the assets a firm requires and, equally important, how these assets may be categorized and then applied. In the strategic paradigm, partnerships come under the umbrella of customer strategies, themselves forming part of a firm's marketing strategy, itself part of generic policy. The choices a firm makes concerning its generic strategy will affect its marketing and, in turn, its customer strategies, so an appreciation of the linkages between these three levels is important to develop a full understanding of the partnership as a tool in customer strategy.

No strategy, however well conceived, exists in a vacuum. Competitive pressures, discontinuities and disturbances, human frailty and other factors all contribute to produce a result different in some way from the intended result and the written plan. These forces can be described as 'degrees of freedom', or the room within which any firm can act before being affected by internal or external dynamics. The nature, strength and dynamism of these forces are different in almost every case, but their impact is always felt in the execution of strategy. Degrees of freedom is not only a concept vital to strategy development in general terms, it is also central to the development and application of marketing strategy. This makes it an essential topic in understanding strategic partnerships.

Last in this chapter we will examine the resources necessary to build successful customer or supplier alliances. Opportunities exist in many industries for firms to create alliances with more than one other organization simultaneously. A word of warning, however: it is difficult enough to build one strategic partnership, so be careful about trying to bite off too big a chunk at once. It would be a better idea to form one or more partnerships and then make them work before trying anything more ambitious. This will also lead to a better informed realization of the resources required.

This is not to say that multifaceted partnerships are impossible, just that they are more difficult. There are two main possibilities: one is for the firm to try to engage several of its suppliers – far easier than several customers – in a partnership; and the other is to bring a supplier, or more than one, into a partnership with the firm and one of its major customers.

Asset classes

When considering what assets a firm possesses, we can begin by dividing them into financial and non-financial assets. The first group can be found on the balance sheet, and are typically such items as:

Financial assets
- Land and buildings
- Plant and machinery
- Vehicles
- Office equipment
- Raw materials
- Debtors
- Cash

And so on ...

However, another class of assets exists alongside these that rarely appears on a balance sheet – intangible assets. It is a fact of business that a firm's intangible assets often have a value equal to, or greater than, its tangible assets. A list of intangible assets would include the following items:

Intangible assets
- Brand names
- People
- Experience
- Competencies
- Information
- Knowhow
- Procedures

And so on ...

In recent years there has been a debate, yet to be fully resolved, about the value of a firm's brands, including its corporate brand, and whether these values should be shown on the balance sheet. Whether or not the Accounting Standards Authority can agree a form acceptable to accountants and to industry remains to be seen. In the meantime, firms will continue to use their assets, tangible and intangible, in the course of their business activities. Both classes of assets are an issue within the partnership context, but of greater significance is the extent to which a firm uses its assets *fully* in doing business with its major customers and suppliers.

Three prime partnership assets

The first step in utilizing intangible assets more fully is to recognize, in the partnership context, what they are. The second consideration is how many prime assets can be used, or are essential, in building strategic partnerships. Currently, and in the majority of instances, two prime assets are used as business-building bridges – the people and the product. The term 'product' is used here to include services.

In the business-to-business arena there is usually face-to-face contact, most frequently between buyers and sellers, but often at other levels and within other disciplines too. This is the intangible, 'people' asset.

In larger firms, the role of major account manager exists, with a variety of job titles, to meet the need of bigger customers for regular personal contact. How to measure the productivity or effectiveness of account managers is a difficult question and one that few firms have been able to resolve satisfactorily. In small to medium-sized firms the role is usually filled by senior people and is therefore less specialized.

Either way, a great deal of effort and cost goes into creating and supporting the role. And as we have seen from trend analyses, there is an increasing risk for the firm that staff will leave to pursue a more interesting or rewarding career elsewhere.

The argument often heard in defence of the current status, where firms place a heavy reliance on their account managers, is that:

■ customers demand it;
■ it's the industry practice;
■ so we might as well have the best.

All this might be true, but it misses a few obvious facts. To begin with, if firms engage in an auction to outbid one another for the best salespeople, only the wealthiest will win. Where does this leave everyone else? Secondly, trend analyses and simple observation suggest that the best people are more and more promiscuous in their employment outlook. If this is true, paying them more is only half the solution. Finding more challenging work, in that sense of reward, is the other half. Finding people more challenging work is not to be pursued as a strategy in its own right, but as part of some larger plan. It will attract cost and therefore must generate more revenue than cost in order to add to the firm's total profit.

Thirdly, salespeople are most effective when they can create and develop good business relationships, but if buyers and sellers are becoming more mobile it makes the skills of relationship management much harder to sustain. In some of the scenarios painted in the Introduction, the amount of face-to-face contact seems likely to diminish even further, making the people argument harder to uphold. And finally, it may be that customers demand it because they do not see the need for anything different; this is the case with many things until we know that an alternative exists.

This is not to say that account managers are not needed, whether they be specialized people in larger firms or more senior managers in smaller firms. Rather, we should be seeking to redefine the need for the current role in the light of what we know about the present and what we believe about the future. In addition, there is a bigger, broader context in which we must see the account management function. It is the application of one of the three key assets, rather than two, that the firm must deploy in its never-ending search for more profitable ways of doing business.

The second asset, the product, has been labelled the 'principal connection' between a supplier of goods or services and its customers. It establishes a *raison d'être* for both parties. Few suppliers hold a - monopolistic position any longer, and those that do are the targets of consumer groups, government and, most crucially, customers. We increasingly see the effects of borderless competition and strategic alliances in individual product-markets.

Except where the product owner can gain protection through patents or intellectual property rights, virtually any product can be copied almost immediately after it has been launched. This makes life difficult enough, but it is made worse by the fact that such copies are not always legal ones. A further complication is that in many cases the product copiers are not competitors, but customers. Again, none of this implies that it is possible or desirable to exist without the product, simply that too heavy a reliance on it can be dangerous.

So if a third prime asset exists, what is it? It is in fact a combination of some of the components shown under the earlier heading of 'intangible assets'. It is best described as 'knowhow', but is really a blend of the firm's beneficial experiences, its ability to move quickly and cost effectively along learning curves, the information it holds and its knowledge. This adds up to knowhow ability. However, it raises two other questions:

■ What is it that we know how to do?
■ How does this benefit us or anyone else?

Answering these questions leads to an understanding that knowhow is a collection of core competencies which a firm has gained over time and which, if applied correctly, can give it an edge over its rivals. In subsequent chapters, we will examine what these core competencies are, what they add up to and how they should be used in the strategic partnership setting. For the moment, however, we should dwell on two other related thoughts:

- Core competencies, adding up to a specific piece of knowhow, are not as transient as salespeople or even products, because systems become embedded in the organization over time and do not fail when one person leaves.
- Core competencies are very difficult to observe from within an organization. From the outside they are opaque. Usually only the results are visible and these are often shrouded in mythology.

The proper classification of prime assets in developing business with customers is therefore the people, the product and the knowhow. It is through a specific bundling and channelling of the application of these assets that strategic partnerships, based on mutually rewarding experiences, can be achieved. One firm's relative advantage over another in this respect limits or enhances each party's freedom of action.

A family of strategies

Every firm has a strategy for its major customers (or so it is claimed) and many have one for their key suppliers as well. A more informative consideration is the order in which these strategies are developed. In too many cases, customer strategies are developed by sales or marketing departments and supplier strategies by purchasing functions, independently of the firm's broader, generic policies. It is as though these latter strategies were being ignored.

The right approach is to begin with generic strategy, since this points the overall direction for the firm in all its activities. Marketing strategy – just one branch of generic strategy, the part related to markets, customers, products and services – can then follow.

Customer strategy comes last, ensuring as far as possible that it fits with the other two. To do otherwise runs the risk of developing customer strategies that are, or will be, in conflict with the firm's overall aims.

Strategy can be subdivided into several forms (see Figure 1.1). We will briefly discuss each in turn, although we will mainly concentrate on the third form, customer strategy. Marketing strategy will be examined later in the chapter when we look at the concept of degrees of freedom. Customer strategy sits within marketing strategy and refers to specific plans developed for individual customers and suppliers. Other parts of the firm's strategy include finance and manufacturing, although they are not considered here.

We will look at generic strategy first, however, since this is the proper setting for both marketing and customer strategies. A firm must establish a strategic context, generally by framing its generic or corporate policy, the overall policy plan for the firm.

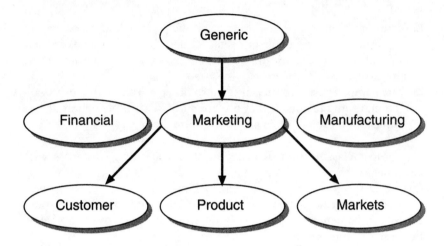

Figure 1.1 A family of strategies

Generic strategy

There are many generic strategies that a firm can follow. The one chosen will depend on the particular firm's external and internal circumstances. All of the actors in its environment must be considered: political, social, economic, demographic and so on. So must the firm's relationship to its competitors, customers and suppliers. This can be seen more clearly in what is usually called the strategic triangle (Figure 1.2).

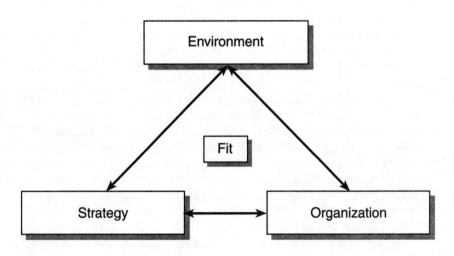

Figure 1.2 The strategic triangle

This model simply illustrates the interconnectedness of the three key factors of the operating environment, the organization within it, and the strategy it has adopted or plans to adopt. It also shows that the three components must 'fit' with one another. Strategy should fulfil at least the following criteria:

■ It should force management to make choices about the allocation of scarce resources.
■ It should direct management to examine the different strategies needed for different business units or, in marketing strategy, different product lines or customer groups.
■ It should find the right strategy that achieves the best fit between the environment and the needs of the organization.
■ It should add wealth to the firm.

Pioneering work by the Boston Consulting Group (BCG) in the USA heralded in a new era in the way managers thought about and planned strategy. In what became known as the growth–share matrix, BCG proposed that, measured against the two dimensions of market growth and relative market share, there are four strategic options for a firm, or for discrete business units within it (see Figure 1.3). 'Relative' market share means relative to the firm's nearest competitor. Later work led to the development of a 'question zone' overlapping two of the original quadrants.

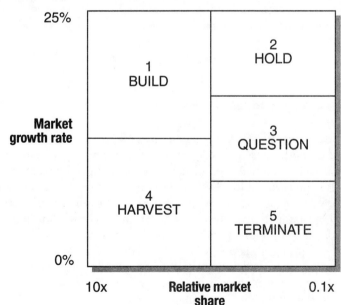

Figure 1.3 BCG growth–share matrix

The analysis aims to show the firm's current strategic position and to provide indicators as to future product-market positions. Of course, if the firm's current position will deliver all its corporate objectives, it will not be necessary to find other opportunities. However, this is not often the case.

Once the initial analysis has been conducted, managers can decide whether other product-market opportunities need to be explored and, if they do, choose the appropriate course of action, fitting it as cleanly as possible to their own specific circumstances. As Igor Ansoff states in *Corporate Strategy*: 'the decision rules for search and evaluation of products and markets are not the same for all firms'. However, once an appropriate search and assessment have been conducted, the resulting answers will give the firm its strategic focus.

We can briefly examine the five strategic focus options in turn. Figure 1.4 considers 'build'.

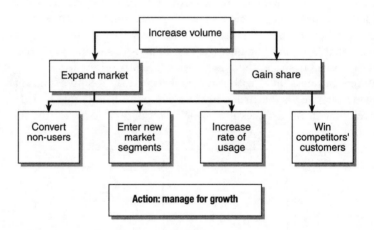

Figure 1.4 Strategic focus 1 – build

Of course, the extent to which managing for growth can be accomplished will depend on both internal factors such as the availability of resources, and external factors such as level of demand and competitor reaction.

Figure 1.5 looks at 'hold'. Defending market share is usually more difficult for market followers, and is especially tricky when faced with a determined, sustainable, penetration pricing attack. Defending margin relies on adopting a policy of continual cost reduction.

Figure 1.6, 'question', is potentially the most difficult set of options. The first hurdle arises in defining the style adopted by the leader; to do this, a full competitive analysis is needed. Trying to short circuit this can easily lead to the wrong choices being made.

As Figure 1.7 shows, before it is possible to manage a business for cash, there must have previously been a policy to develop so-called cash

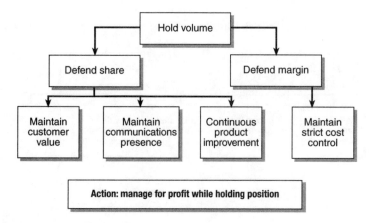

Figure 1.5 Strategic focus 2 – hold

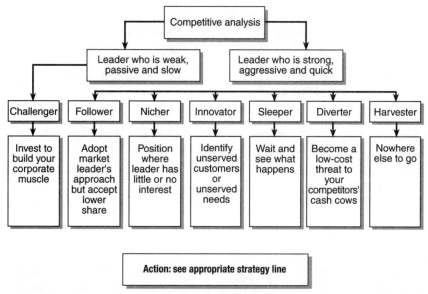

Figure 1.6 Strategic focus 3 – question

cows. This implies a well-considered portfolio management approach.

Figure 1.8 describes the focus option of 'terminate'. Liquidation or divestiture of assets can be phased or immediate, depending on the severity of the situation. Emotion can easily cloud managers' perspectives and corporate history is littered with wrecks that ought to have been withdrawn from service. However, human optimism sometimes overcomes objective analysis.

Partnership strategies usually come within the orbit of strategic focus 1, build, and are most often are geared towards the growth of volume through market expansion.

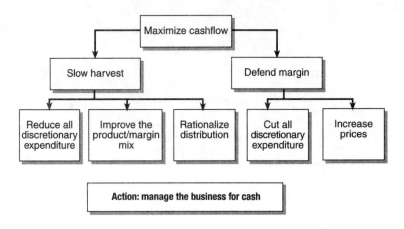

Figure 1.7 Strategic focus 4 – harvest

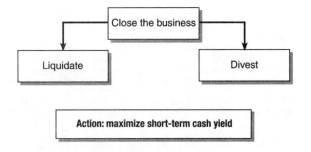

Figure 1.8 Strategic focus 5 – terminate

Marketing strategy

Usually enshrined in a written marketing plan, marketing strategy fulfils the same purpose and function as generic strategy, but at a different level. In setting its marketing policy, the firm is stating how it will create the best fit between its products and services, markets and customers within those markets. Additionally, the plan will contain statements concerning trends and what they mean, competitors, consumers or end-users, trade customers, marketing channels and budgets. Generic strategy will have set the overall direction, now marketing strategy must turn that focus into specific product-market plans.

There are three broad choices, shown in Figure 1.9. As we shall see, none conveys absolute freedom.

The individual components shown in the model are only meant to be illustrative of those the firm would consider in making choices about marketing strategy. Selection lies between competing on cost advantage,

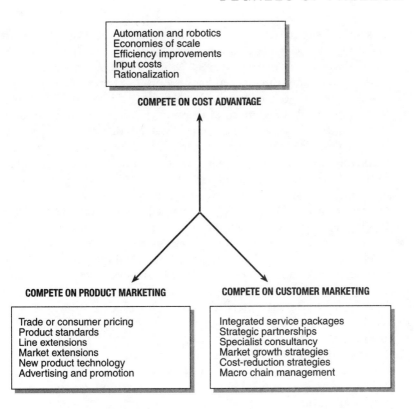

Figure 1.9 Strategic degrees of freedom

product marketing or customer marketing. To claim that selections can be made from each option, thus creating a hybrid, 'best of three worlds', is an exercise in self-delusion. The appropriate answer in each firm's case will depend on a combination of factors impossible to replicate here; what is important is to be clear that there is a requirement to select the one approach that is more appropriate to the firm and its circumstances than either of the other two. This does not mean that all the examples in the box chosen need to be applied, only those that fit the firm's knowhow and other capabilities.

The following examples will help illustrate the model and its application:

■ Coca-Cola competes heavily on product marketing. The company made the decision to divest itself of its biggest distributor in the USA. It was reported that this was done largely as a means of enabling management to focus more clearly on manufacturing. Yet the move could be seen as giving Coca-Cola even greater freedom in product marketing, in that it freed up cash and management time to devote to achieving an even stronger product emphasis.

■ It is sometimes possible for individual components from more than one option to be pursued in tandem, so long as they follow the rule given above about appropriateness. A firm might choose to invest in acquisitions as a means of making new products and simultaneously concentrate more heavily on product innovation. For example, Microsoft has obtained much of its product range, and many innovative ideas, from a series of acquisitions. A focus on product marketing has led the firm into a virtuous circle, where its original product-marketing focus generated enough money to invest in acquiring other firms. It is not vital, or probably even wise, to try to manage too many components of the model at once; it is better to be selective and try to manage a smaller number in a more telling way that will deliver superior performance to your customers in a form they recognize.

■ Direct Line became a low-cost operator in the UK insurance market by eliminating links in the distribution chain. Industry observers have pointed out the similarity between Direct Line's product portfolio and those of its competitors, so a focus on product marketing would have been difficult; casual observation of its marketing strategy would seem to rule out customer marketing, since its customers are not the insurance trade but consumers.

■ Northern Foods is a very successful manufacturing business, much better known in the UK grocery trade than among consumers. It set out to become a retailer own-brand producer and placed a heavy emphasis on this strategy.

Degrees of freedom

The great difficulty with most strategic approaches lies in turning theory into practice. This is probably equally true of each of the three forms of marketing strategy discussed above. Sometimes the difficulty occurs because managers do not know how, although the amount of advice that has been published on this subject should rule that out. Frequently, it is because there seems to be insufficient time and too much pressure to do all the analysis necessary. Occasionally, it is because managers 'just know what to do and how to do it', making a written plan appear unnecessary.

Perhaps a combination of these factors is also true. Certainly, it is a common commercial reality that there is too much work and never enough time in which to do it properly. And yet running a business without sound planning procedures is more of an adventure than it should be, significantly increasing the risk of failure. Risk cannot be completely eliminated, but it is foolish to manage an enterprise by ignoring it. Understanding the risks facing a firm at a given time through use of the proper tools, and then taking the appropriate steps at both the planning and execution stages, is a much more sensible way forward, even though it can be more time consuming.

'Freedom to act' is a relative concept and applies at all three strategic levels. Managers only have freedom to act where certain circumstances apply. There are forces in every environment that limit the freedom to act of everyone in the market. Competitors often limit actions, as does the availability of internal resources, but the most important criterion in customer marketing is customer acceptance or resistance.

Instruments are required that give managers a reliable estimate of the likely degree of resistance and acceptance for the potential policy, irrespective of the level of strategy at which it occurs. One approach is to use weighted analysis.

To bring this concept to life, imagine that we are considering specific customer strategies and that we need insight into which parts of the proposed plan will meet either of the two customer forces and what weight we should give to them. We could proceed as follows.

Our first step, of course, is to see every customer as being uniquely different, however subtly. Recognizing this means that we have moved to thinking about specific customer marketing strategy, rather than considering customers as groups in a general market segmentation sense.

Next, we must determine a list of strategy options under consideration, for example:

- Trade dealing terms (change to benefit the firm).
- Customer service levels (change to reduce cost).
- Partnerships (type yet to be determined).
- Value chain analysis (type yet to be determined).
- Function planting (take over a section of customer's business).
- Sales and marketing organization (different to current).

This list of possible options, relating to a specific customer, can now be given weightings (see Table 1.1).

The example demonstrates the following:

- The supplier believes the three most important strategies with this customer are a positive change in dealing terms, some form of partnership or an analysis of the value chain.
- There is high customer resistance to changes in dealing terms that are seen to favour the supplier, customer service levels and function planting. In the last two cases, customer confusion may be the reason. However, due to the low level of customer acceptance to a change in dealing terms, it scores only 2.0. Function planting scores even lower, while a rating of 4.5 is given to changing customer service levels.
- Partnership and value chain analysis have the highest customer acceptance scores and both have a reasonably good resistance score.

Table 1.1 Weighting of options

Option	W	R	A	–	+
Trade dealing terms	20	9	1	18.0	2.0
Customer service levels	15	7	3	10.5	4.5
Partnership	20	4	5	8.0	10.0
Value chain analysis	20	5	5	10.0	10.0
Function planting	10	7	1	7.0	1.0
Sales/Mktg organization	15	3	2	4.5	3.0
	100				

W = Weighting
R = Resistance
A = Acceptance
– = Resistance score multiplied by the weighting
+ = Acceptance score multiplied by the weighting

■ Making a judicious combination of the two factors of resistance and acceptance, there is a relatively better likelihood of success if the firm pursues either of these policies. Its chances of success weaken sharply when dealing terms or function planting is considered.

There are two inputs into this analysis: the first is from the firm's side, the second from the customer's viewpoint. The latter is vital if the actions proposed are to be rooted in reality and are to meet with better than average chances of success. The only real difficulty in this approach lies in persuading customers to take part in the development of your strategy for their business. How this can be achieved will be dealt with in depth in subsequent chapters, but is encapsulated in the concept and practice of partnership.

The factors that help determine whether a firm can translate strategic theory or wishes into reality can easily be overlooked or given insufficient weight. Moving from hope to promise means balancing three key factors. These are resources, willpower and freedom to act, and they overlap (Figure 1.10).

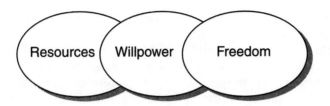

Figure 1.10 Translating theory into reality

Resources

There are never enough resources to do everything, so choices have to be made. This is a given for most managers most of the time. However, one of the principal functions of strategic planning, at any level, is to highlight where the inevitably scarce resources should be targeted.

The resources usually considered during the planning cycle are money, materials and people, but, as we have seen, knowhow is another crucial ingredient. We can define knowhow as a set of core competencies which the firm has learned, which it can apply to its business to create superior performance and which it can teach to subsequent generations of managers and staff.

It is a general principle of resources planning, particularly when applied to money, that:

■ costs will be greater than budgeted for and will arise earlier than planned; and
■ income will be smaller than planned and will come in late.

Another common difficulty, probably caused in part by the short-term nature of western stock markets, is in planning sufficient resources to get the business plan or project off the ground, but not enough to sustain it if something goes wrong.

Resource planning is always a difficult matter to get right and there are few easy solutions. Something on which almost everyone seems to agree, however, is that a well-considered strategy makes it easier than would otherwise be the case.

Willpower

Inability to initiate action is rarely the fault of planning; more often it arises because not enough management willpower exists to take sometimes risky decisions, occasionally in cases where the risk cannot be assessed properly and especially when framed in an uncertain future. Turning thought and analysis into clear and unified action is made harder if managers in all parts of the firm are all fighting their corners when resources are handed out.

Willpower can make the difference between strategic success and failure. Many good plans have come undone because of a lack of management will to see them through. The reverse argument is probably untrue, however. Poor plans will not often succeed, even if dosed with liberal quantities of management willpower.

Freedom to act

And last, plans can fail to be executed properly or at all because of the firm's freedom of action – or lack of it. This is a crucial consideration, particularly at the planning stage. It is quite possible for managers to develop a good plan which works in theory but which fails in practice. Of course, there can be many reasons for this, but a major one is that the firm's freedom to act was not thought through in the right way during the planning stage. In other words, plans are drawn up with insufficient weight given to the pressures, current or future, which will impinge on the plan when it is put into effect.

Pressures come from several sources. A further way of examining a firm's room for manoeuvre can be seen in Figure 1.11. In this example, institutional shareholders can hold back the development of strategy in action by demanding higher dividends or changes in management. As a result, the firm has only 80 per cent freedom to act, because higher dividend payments mean there is less capital available, reducing freedom by 20 per cent. There is a potential acquirer on the horizon as well and this further constrains action, funds being diverted to a defence. A foreign government has placed a tariff on the import of certain products and our firm, along with others, has fallen foul of this. It is believed that the level of demand for the firm's product could be increased by another 15 per cent and no doubt this would be reflected, along with its costs, in the marketing plan. The firm has some slack, about 30 per cent, in its physical production capacity. End-users in the main market are economically constrained at present. Competitors are powerful. Suppliers are thought likely to be able to keep pace with what looks like slow progress. Importantly, customer acceptance is believed to be high. Resources, as always, are scarce. The other internal constraint, inertia, also acts to limit the firm's freedom.

Managers would consider each of these factors, or the ones most appropriate to the firm's situation, making a judgement about the level of pressure applied by each and therefore its freedom to act. Some of these factors will be beyond the firm's control, such as foreign government action; others will be within the orbit of influence and it is on these that managers should focus their attention.

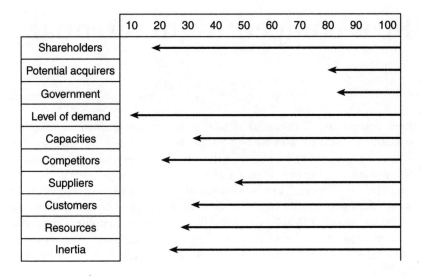

Figure 1.11 Freedom to act

Customer strategy

Customer strategy incorporates supplier strategies. These resemble customer plans in at least one respect, namely, that they usually deal with one firm at a time. Every firm is a link in a microeconomic chain that usually comprises at least three links: supplier, firm and customer. Value chains stretch further in each direction, back to raw material inputs and forward to consumers and end-users.

The remainder of this book is concerned with one particular aspect of customer strategy – partnerships. Reference to the strategic partnership model, discussed in detail in Chapter 3, will be helpful in identifying the steps of the process, as well as the many nuances involved in building a strategic alliance.

Real competitive differential

Real competitive differential (RCD) is based on knowing or having something – including knowing how to do something – that nobody else knows or has and being able to use it to gain a commercial advantage. Simultaneously, the firm must seek to protect this proprietary knowhow from others. 'Others' can sometimes include customers, for example where the firm supplies customer-branded goods, usually in fast-moving consumer goods (FMCG) markets. In such cases, customers not only seek to copy the physical product, but also to capture the proprietary knowhow that manufactures and markets the product under its owner's brand name.

In Chapter 1, we explored the idea that firms need three legs on which to build a strategic platform: the product or service that is at the core of the business; the people who make, distribute, sell and service it; and a set of core competencies. Bundled together in a specific way, these core competencies can become real competitive differential. In this chapter, we will try to identify a method for realizing a specific set of competencies, moulding them into a unique 'product' and using this to signal a difference that is superior. To achieve real superiority, the differential must be recognized by customers as offering a greater benefit, or set of benefits, than is currently the case. The benefit must be sufficient to attract customers to the firm when they have other choices, and to retain their loyalty over time.

There are many ways in which firms can achieve a competitive advantage over their rivals:

■ On a macro scale, in the pharmaceuticals industry it is common for firms to be given lengthy patents to protect their branded knowledge. This prevents others from offering copies until the patent runs out.
■ On a micro scale, in the mortgage market banks and building societies offer up-front incentives, but simultaneously lock consumers into staying with them for several years, thus achieving a form of loyalty as well as establishing switching costs.
■ In the early twentieth century, British regional railway operators built physical distribution systems that monopolized the track and shut out competitors until they were nationalized after the Second World War.
■ John Deere developed hydrostatic transmission, enabling large earth-moving vehicles to turn in their own length. This provided a competitive advantage until it was copied by the Japanese.

■ Electronics giant Philips developed the handheld calculator, triggering off a new market and, later, new industries such as handheld games and business applications.

■ John Grisham uses his training as a US attorney – as well as an obvious gift for writing – to create interesting stories about law and justice.

■ Southwest Airlines has carved out a growing share of US air travel by being the lowest-cost operator, an advantage based on its avoidance of high-cost hubs.

■ Channel 9 in Australia became the number 1 television sports channel by 'modernizing' sports coverage, previously considered tired and outdated. It attracted significantly higher advertising revenues in the process.

Real competitive differential also has to be difficult to copy, since this gives it longevity and reduces its cost over time. It is expensive enough to develop any form of advantage, costlier still when it has to be redefined and reshaped every year or two. Most commercial advantages are either visible at first glance or can be discovered through a more thorough competitive analysis. This does not necessarily mean that the advantage will be copied, but visibility does make copying simpler for those competitors and customers who want to do it. Ideally, we need a form of competitive differential that is known or owned exclusively by our firm and that is simultaneously opaque. Finally, it must be understood widely within the firm and capable of being translated into action. A combination of these three factors – exclusivity, opacity and action focus – makes the differential real. Anything less is fool's gold.

Therefore the aim, as we begin assembling a set of core competencies, is to create something unique, which is authoritative, which works and which is affordable.

Looked at in this way, we can see why it is so difficult for anyone to copy Disney theme parks (Figure 2.1). The core product is 'good clean fun for all the family'; understanding this enables the firm to build on this foundation whenever it is considering a new theme park or updates to existing parks. Of course, it has an advantage in owning many of the Disney characters, but corporate history is littered with firms which have owned valuable assets and never understood how to use them.

Understanding assets in this way also makes it easier for the firm to concentrate on learning how to manage a relatively small number of competencies. The number will differ from one case to another, but it is their specific arrangement that makes them unique.

McDonald's real product is 'food and fun for all the family' (Figure 2.2). This is why its competitors have such a hard time copying what it does so well. They think McDonald's is in the hamburger business. Of

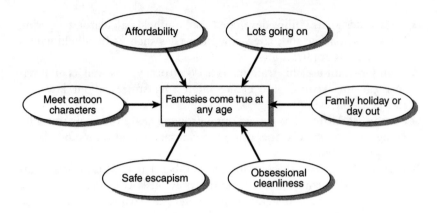

Figure 2.1 Walt Disney theme parks

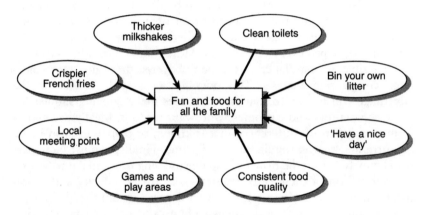

Figure 2.2 McDonald's restaurants

course, its real business is making money. Its real strategy is to have a consistent brand that is extremely difficult to observe – because, although the individual components are visible to anyone, their arrangement into a particular cluster is not – and that it uses many of its assets in a unique way. This makes it very difficult, almost impossible, to copy. McDonald's real product is an amalgam of the way it uses its assets, simply defined and well understood, at least by its employees. Its customers might not recognize the asset map shown here, but they have no difficulty in recognizing the McDonald's experience and in telling it apart from its many rivals.

Let us examine this strategy in more detail:

■ Everyone in the restaurant business aims to have clean toilets and some accomplish this consistently, so there is nothing very special about that.

■ McDonald's has thicker milkshakes than most, although those at Hardee's are probably thicker.

■ Ronald McDonald is the character used in advertisements to attract young families for children's parties. Play trains and other party accoutrements are provided.

■ Restaurants, other than drive-throughs, are located in town centres and are brightly lit, attractive meeting points for young people.

■ The menu is kept tight and controllable to achieve maximum consistency in line with food quality aims.

■ If anyone had suggested 25 years ago that customers could be persuaded to clean up and bin their own litter when leaving their tables, most people would have said they were crazy.

■ 'Have a nice day' and, more recently, 'Missing you already' are just the spoken words which accompany the McDonald's welcome. Staff are trained to reflect this by appropriate eye contact and body posture.

■ Crispy French Fries add another ingredient to the cocktail of McDonald's difference.

Arguably, McDonald's is the world's most successful restaurant operator and its brand is mobile. It is truly a global player. Its closest comparable rival, Burger King, is backed by one of the world's wealthiest firms, yet seems unable to close the gap. For a more detailed discussion of McDonald's core brand, see Chris Steward, *Managing Major Accounts* (1996).

Searching for clues

The process of assembling a set of core competencies – the sum of which is specific knowhow, the advantage of which is customer-perceived superiority of performance and the benefit of which is greater wealth creation – is painstaking but worthwhile. We can begin hunting for clues to a firm's RCD by examining the three circles in Figure 2.3.

'Understood' does not necessarily mean that something is understood now, but also that understanding can flow from investigation. Example components of the three circles are shown in Table 2.1.

This list is by no means exhaustive, but serves to indicate two important elements. First, the way in which end-users or consumers see the firm and its products is not the way in which trade customers see them, and is almost certainly different from the way in which the firm sees itself and its products. Each of these perceptions is valid, just different. And secondly, the three circles cannot be separated as the firm goes about its business. Whether consciously in day-to-day decision making or not, managers must take continual account of the changing needs of consumers or end-users, of their trade customers and of their own needs.

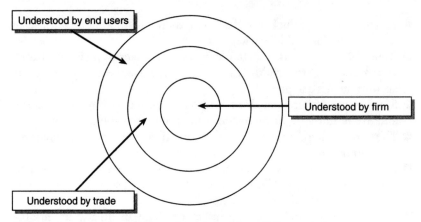

Figure 2.3 Three circles of competitive differential

Table 2.1 Components of the three circles

Understood by end users	Understood by trade	Understood by firm
Advertising	Promotion capability	A&P management
Product/brand names	Technical specifications	Branding
Quality perceptions	Quality assurance	Technology knowhow
Place of availability	Parts management	Logistics knowhow
Price	Dealing terms	Customer management

Of equal importance is the idea that we can use this type of listing methodology to help search for areas in which the firm already has a core competency, or can and should obtain one by whatever means, using this as one building block in its construction of real competitive differential. Given that the different needs of two different types of customer must be managed, and that they sometimes co-exist painfully for the supplier, it is management's task to resolve these inherent conflicts through the application of its various strategies, while at the same time building and sustaining its commercial edge.

Remembering that we are dealing here with trade customers, and assuming for a moment that we are dealing with a firm supplying FMCG customers where advertising and promotion (A&P) is a key issue, we can take one example from the list (Table 2.2).

The question that immediately arises is this: how can the application of an advertising and promotion strategy be used to develop a customer-perceived superiority, while simultaneously building real competitive differential for the firm?

The trade customer generally wants less advertising, which it considers poorly targeted and wasteful, and more customer-specific promo-

Table 2.2 FMCG example

Understood by end users	Understood by trade	Understood by firm
Advertising	Promotion capability	A&P management

tions. It has greater control over this type of expenditure and believes that it benefits directly from money spent in this way. The supplier usually wants both: advertising because it is widely held that it creates, or at least reinforces, brand equity; and promotions because they satisfy the needs of the trade customer. For most suppliers in this position it is a matter of balance, and a good deal of management thought and time goes into striking the right balance. These discussions miss a central point, however, which is the extent to which promotional activity works at all.

In the early 1990s, Professors Ehrenberg, Hammond and Goodhardt studied the subject of FMCG trade promotions in the UK, USA, Germany and Japan. They produced what is probably the seminal work on the subject and one containing many valuable lessons as well as raising additional questions. Their study destroyed or severely weakened some of the accepted wisdom surrounding trade promotions, in particular that a higher-volume baseline is achieved following the campaign, that this produces a springboard for the next one and that promotions have a brand-building role. These authors found no evidence for these claims or for several other promotional myths, despite examining over 100 leading brands in 16 product fields. They concluded: 'Our study has shown that consumer promotions for established FMCG brands appear generally to have no after-effect on sales or on repeat buying loyalty.'

In reality, the real volume of hard, tangible evidence that exists on this subject is tiny compared with the wealth of activity taking place. And we are not talking about insignificant sums of money. The UK passed the halfway mark some years ago and now has a bigger share of A&P money devoted to promotion than advertising. It followed the USA in this respect. Figures are very difficult to establish, but annual expenditure in the UK of at least £2 billion is probably close to the mark and the US market is much larger. Anecdotal evidence of promotional success is easier to come by, but it is based on flimsy scientific rigour. In many cases, and apart from keeping a powerful trade customer satisfied, nobody knows what benefits have in fact accrued from such campaigns.

Let us return to our original question. How can the application of a firm's A&P strategy be used to develop a customer-perceived superiority, while simultaneously building real competitive differential for the firm? For the moment, we will explore the question by posing other questions.

Of the dozens that would be of interest to our investigation, here are some very important supplementary ones:

- What is the cost of building stock, including machine changeover time, inventory financing cost, inability to make other product on the same machine at the same time, salesforce selling time, promotional literature and so on?
- What is the cost of lost orders resulting from a lack of activity after volume peaks?
- What is the cost of consumer confusion regarding the real price of the product and their capacity to wait until the next promotion before buying again?
- How can competitor reaction best be assessed in advance of a promotion, and what is the real cost to the firm of buying back any volume or share it may have lost during competitor promotions?
- What is the role of promotions in building long-term consumer brand loyalty; indeed, is there such a phenomenon?

If these questions seem rather difficult to answer, try some easier ones:

- What is the best way for customer and supplier to evaluate the relative success or failure of promotions?
- What is the contribution to margin of each type of promotion mounted, at different campaign seasons, in different geographic markets, by customer, for each product or brand?
- From the trade customer's perspective, are individual promotions intended to build external or internal traffic, or transactions, or store brand loyalty, or what?
- Apart from bringing forward volume that would probably arise less expensively anyway, what are the firm's objectives in mounting promotions?

Few of these questions would elicit swift or objective responses. The entire structure of FMCG promotions seems to exist because of pressure from powerful trade customers or pressure from marketing and salespeople to see more sales in the short term. In other words, promotions are tactical tools and should not be confused with the firm's strategy.

None of this implies that firms in FMCG markets can or should eliminate promotional activity. However, a reduction of just a few percentage points would provide additional resources to spend in other areas. And if these other areas were believed to be more beneficial in the long run, it would be a sensible policy to adopt.

In relation to the main question we have been discussing, our enquiry appears to have thrown up two possibilities: one is to spend ever more money doing more and more promotions, and the other is to divert some of the money into longer-term brand building. This is not in this case an individual product or service brand, but the brand of the firm itself. However, what if both tactical and strategic goals could be satisfied at once? Would that not be the best way of all? It is realistically possible. To achieve it, the firm must pursue two goals at once:

1 It must become an expert, as distinct from a practitioner, in the art of sales promotion. It must develop an understanding, based on lengthy and detailed enquiries into the questions posed earlier, of the proper role of promotions. It must then utilize this knowledge in a specific way with selected trade customers. Selected means exactly that. This knowledge will be so powerful, so valuable, that it would be foolish to give it away to everyone, just as foolish as giving away any other of the firm's assets. Thinking customers will see it as a benefit because it may help them redefine the promotional role in their brand-development strategy.
2 Simultaneously with the acquisition of this knowledge, the firm must begin to reduce, by a few percentage points, the amount of money it spends on promotions. In practice, and in the proper context, this can be done with the agreement and support of the trade customer. The right context is a strategic partnership.

We now have one of the ovals in a firm-specific set of competencies for an organization in the FMCG supply market (Figure 2.4).

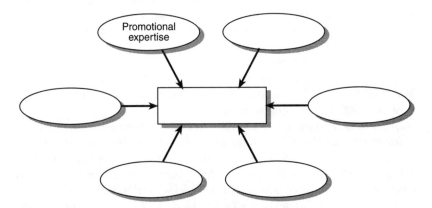

Figure 2.4 Firm-specific competencies

Let us now turn our attention to a different question, in a different industry situation, and consider how this might be used to develop real competitive differential. Take the case of a manufacturer of automotive parts, whose customer is a vehicle manufacturer (Table 2.3).

Table 2.3 Automotive example

Understood by end-users	Understood by trade	Understood by firm
Place of availability	Parts management	Logistics knowhow

Once again, we have one issue seen from three different perspectives. Here though, the end-user and the trade are just different departments or functions within one firm. 'Trade' refers to the buying process, 'end-user' means the installation process. The end-user is mainly concerned with the availability of the part, both at the point of production and in the inventory chain, and sequencing this with the volume and speed of the production process. The buying department has different priorities. Its chief concerns surround the price – balanced against the quality, stockholding costs, and availability and quality of suppliers. It must try to balance the needs of the end-user against those of the firm as a whole. Buyers see a parts-management chain stretching from the supplier to their internal production point.

The supplier sees a value chain beginning with the need for the part and looping back to its raw material suppliers. The supplier forms another link in this chain, as do the buying and production departments of its customer. In fact, each time there is a transaction concerning the product, anywhere in its life, it forms a new link in a chain of events. These links cover raw materials sourcing, including mining, physical distribution, space utilization, materials handling, stock control, plant layout, production systems, speed of flow, quality of management, and supply and demand management. The chain has five main components: materials, labour, overheads, time and capital. Every transaction link in the value chain has costs, both direct and indirect, fixed and variable, and understanding the interplay between events and their cost is the key to unlocking value-adding secrets.

We can now rephrase our earlier question: in which component, or components, of the value chain are we really expert, or can become really expert, so delivering greater value to our customers and ourselves? Of course, the answer cannot be defined here – it will depend on many circumstances, some of which will be specific to the firm.

As an example, however, we can imagine a situation in which a firm takes its existing knowledge of logistics management and adds to this more specific knowledge concerning space utilization and plant layout, two related topics within the overall subject. In boxes of raw materials and finished product, on pallets, in vehicles and in warehouses and factories, the cost of unused space costs the same as the space being used.

For example, the space above the machine costs the same as the space it occupies. Similarly, the unused space between pallet heads and the vehicle roof costs the same as that occupied by the pallet itself. In some cases, 'lost space' cannot be used, for example for reasons of safety. In many other cases, however, the balance between the space that is used and what is lost can be redressed. All five factors above can play a part; for instance, the amount of time that space is unused will have an impact on the capital needed to finance it.

The potential for adding value is tremendous. While this whole subject has been studied in depth in recent years and some major advances have been achieved, not enough has been made of the potential for using new knowledge to create and sustain commercial partnerships. This is simply another context for what we already know, or can learn.

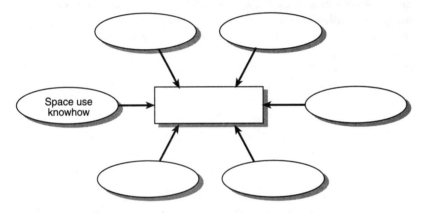

Figure 2.5 Further firm-specific competencies

To complete either of the two knowhow models proposed above, we would proceed in the same way, namely, by examining customer needs, current competencies or ones we could learn and forming the answers into a unique customer proposition. There is no hard-and-fast rule for the number of ovals represented, though it is likely to be five, six or seven. The centre rectangle is completed last, once the outer markers can be seen. Remember that defining the model is only the first step: learning how to manage it internally and demonstrating it to customers externally are the real tests.

Learning the model

The process of creating a real competitive differential model is an iterative one. It takes time and should be worked on by a group selected for the purpose. Cross-functional groups often work best, sometimes with a diagonal slice to include managers and staff at different levels. Whichever approach is preferred, it must have the active support of top management. Without this, it can become an exercise in futility that produces nothing more than a wish list. It is generally better to have top management participation in the model-creation process; indeed, some would argue that top management alone should do the work.

Once the design phase has been completed, we can move to internalization. This means taking the model and, more importantly, the message contained within it and teaching it to everyone in the firm. In recent years, firms have generally become very adept at taking strategic messages from the boardroom to the shopfloor, and the methodology needed here is identical. As in other cases, the message must be communicated clearly and unambiguously, with managers and staff given the opportunity to question and clarify understanding. At regular intervals afterwards, the authors or those tasked with the responsibility should check that the message has been implemented and that it is working.

The message must contain the 'how to', that is, how to translate a theoretical diagram into commercial practice. In order to achieve this level of understanding throughout the firm, top management should work with others to define, in words, what 'promotional expertise' or 'space knowhow' actually means. Practical descriptions, and sometimes checklists, help people grasp the concept fairly easily, but role plays and discussion groups can also help. Patience is a virtue in business as everywhere else in life, and top management will need some patience to see their colleagues up the learning curve.

Very often, all the knowledge needed resides somewhere in the firm. What are required are the time, methodology and willpower to dig it out, reform it and apply it to the model. On other occasions, outside assistance must be sought. An example might be where the firm needs a specific piece of knowledge or skill to apply to what it already knows or has. This approach must be accompanied by an audit to establish what core competencies the firm possesses now and where the gaps are, if any.

The internal process can be visualized as comprising the steps shown in Figure 2.6.

There remains the crucial external element of demonstrating real competitive differential to trade customers. This is the fifth and final step in the process (Figure 2.7). In practice, demonstrating and testing take place together, because it is impossible to demonstrate RCD without testing against the only reality that counts – the customer.

Demonstrating the model

The components of a firm's real competitive differential remain its property, its asset, and the firm has every right as well as sound business reasons for not divulging its RCD to anyone, customers and suppliers included. There is little benefit to be gained from such an explanation in

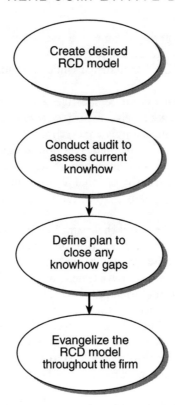

Figure 2.6 Learning the model

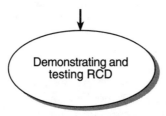

Figure 2.7 The final step

any case, as the customer and supplier will only be interested in what benefits might accrue to them from their commercial relationships. This is the business credo whether an RCD exists or not.

Used properly, a firm's RCD becomes its personality, the way it is recognized by other firms or, more accurately, individuals in other firms. When a firm understands its RCD and how to use it uniquely, it affects the way it does business. This is often in small, hardly perceptible ways, but when taken together with more noticeable changes it forms a new perspective. There are two angles of vision on this: one internal and the other external. Mastering the internal perspective enables managers first to grasp and then to teach the personality of the firm and how it differs from before and from other firms. Understanding this means knowing 'who we are'.

There is also the external perspective. As buyers scan the horizon for suppliers, they often perceive a host of identical offerings. The firms making up a particular supply market may be very different from one another, but that may not be the perception of buyers, who generally like standardization. It is simpler when things can be compared to one another on an apparently rational basis. This helps evaluation and decision making. It makes matters more certain when surrounded by uncertainty.

When goods, services and their suppliers are thought of as being very similar or identical, the key criterion on which decisions can be made is price. Price has the advantage of being highly measurable. It becomes the buyer's stock in trade and, over time, suppliers learn that price is a critical issue. Firms wishing to supply these buyers must be willing to enter into discussions on price, or they will be regarded as unhelpful. Every time such a discussion or negotiation takes place, it reinforces the buyer's belief that price is the most important variable. For those firms that have achieved true lowest-cost status, this is manna from heaven. For the remainder, life hovers between being difficult and becoming a nightmare.

A vicious circle is being created and to break out of it usually requires some effort. Developing real competitive differential offers a break-out opportunity. Fully realized, a firm can stand out and genuinely be seen by others as being different. However, 'different' on its own is of little value unless it is accompanied by something more tangible.

Few professional buyers are attracted by a difference; most are attracted by a benefit, the acquisition of which can mean gaining a business advantage. It seems clear therefore that an RCD, if it is to mean anything, must offer the firm's suppliers and customers a tangible benefit. It is this realization among customers and suppliers that in itself begins the process of standing out from the rest. The distinction will not last long, however, unless it is quickly turned into something more concrete.

The tangibility lies in the way in which the firm does business, at least with certain suppliers and customers. The process of creating a map of real competitive differential, and developing an understanding of what it means and how to use it, changes the way in which the firm acts. The product of this work is a manner of doing business. It must be recognizably different, and superior to, the way in which competitors do business. Added to the firm's physical products or services and its people, it can signal distinctive superiority to the market. The hoped-for response to this signal is an understanding among buyers that 'we know them when we see them and we like what we see'.

The benefits to customers, suppliers and the firm can only become evident once theory is put into practice. To achieve this, a specific business relationship must be created in which the RCD can thrive. Several such opportunities can be identified, but it is on one of these, strategic partnerships, that we shall now focus our thinking.

Strategic partnerships

Forms of partnership

There is no absolute necessity to have strategic partnerships with major customers or suppliers, any more than there is to have a generic strategy for the business as a whole. However, most people would agree that generic strategy helps in many ways, not least in defining, shaping and helping to deliver superior corporate performance.

It is similar with partnership strategy, although here we are focusing on individual major customers or suppliers, with the emphasis on the former. These are the customers who, in so many cases, represent 20 per cent of our customer base but as much as 80 per cent of our turnover or profit. Most of these customers are driven by the same business imperatives as everyone else. They are working hard to differentiate their firm and its brand from their competitors, to drive costs down and margins up, to find profitable new products and services, and to create superior returns on capital invested.

One of the ways in which the more professional and forward-looking firms try to achieve this is by working with selected suppliers in a closer relationship than is usual with others. Suppliers can either become one of these favoured suppliers or remain on the outside with the majority – there is no middle way. The same is true of a firm's relations with its suppliers. The traditional buyer–seller relationship can be continued, with varying degrees of success, or the supplier can try to find better ways of working together with major customers for mutual benefit.

There are many forms of partnership: mergers, takeovers and informal alliances are all variants. There are other forms too, including 'false partnerships'. These exist when the term is used non-authentically by one side, usually the party intending to take most and give the least. Some of these firms use the word 'partnership' as a code for gaining margin at their supplier's expense. This is sharing what value already exists, although on a rather more inequitable basis than before, rather than any attempt to create new value. The amount of value to be shared is, to some degree, limited by the supplier's gross margin – the supplier normally being unwilling to sell at below cost.

The extent to which this can realistically become the foundation for a true partnership is open to debate. Any supplier would be wise to consider whether these are the firms with which it wants to enter into a partnership with long-term objectives, or whether it would prefer to trade with these customers on a more traditional basis. Everyone has a choice.

True strategic partnerships

'True' partnerships can sometimes be strategic – they are always authentic. True strategic partnerships only exist where both parties have demonstrated actual commitment, through action as well as words. It is the difference between a marriage and a one-night stand. The sign of a true strategic partnership is demonstrable, tangible commitment. Customers unwilling or unable to demonstrate what they say is commitment to a partnership should be treated with caution.

Of course, this demonstrable commitment is a two-way street. It must also be demonstrated by the supplying firm, and this means having the willingness to demonstrate commitment in a real and tangible way. In practice, this desire on the part of a supplier is very likely to be the case in any case.

A partnership is only a true strategic partnership when both sides give something and both sides get something in return.

True strategic partners are willing to make compromises to get the best deal for both. To achieve this, it is essential to share. A number of things must be shared, among which the key elements are:

■ *Data*. Sharing data is vital to bridge gaps in comprehension as well as being proof of partnership. Joint analysis leads to shared understanding, and shared understanding leads to purposeful action.
■ *Policies*. Suppliers' strategies are commonly at variance with those of their major customers. Strategic partnerships do not seek to change the overall policies of either partner, but to harmonize a specific set of strategies inside a partnership, while at the same time bringing about a deeper knowledge of each other's aims. Real partners should be able to agree and to differ, and to be open about these matters at the same time.
■ *Processes*. These may be technical, administrative, procedural, knowledge or skill based. The aim of sharing processes is to achieve best practice. The method is to transfer best practice from one partner to another through a variety of systemic approaches.
■ *Ideas*. Innovation is one of the great gateways to business success, now and in the future. It can be developed in many ways, one of which is to create a 'positive creative friction' between two firms which, from their respective positions, see the world in different ways. The energy is almost always there, but it is static. It needs the conduit of a partnership to bring it to life.
■ *Costs*. As the partnership develops, costs specific to it will arise. It is unrealistic as well as unfair to expect that one partner should bear all of these costs alone. In the concept of risk and reward, the two go hand in hand. True partners therefore share costs on a basis seen to be equitable to both sides.

■ *Margin*. The same argument applies here. Two ideas are central to the issue: that the concept of mutuality rests on a fair sharing of burden and benefit alike, and that the core purpose of a business alliance is to create extra margin. To attain the former means that the additional margin created must be shared equitably, and to achieve the latter requires the framing of an agreed programme of work within the partnership.

One of the ways in which a firm can demonstrate its commitment to a true partnership is to begin by recognizing that each of its major customers is a market in its own right. Each one is subtly different – often in many ways – to its apparently identical industry neighbours. Stating this to customers and recognizing it by practical, demonstrable means are not the same thing. We will examine later how these ideas can be tested and validated.

True strategic partnerships can be difficult to create and are often resource hungry, so they should be reserved for the relatively small number of major customers which are willing to enter an equitable relationship, and with which sufficient new value can be created to make the effort worthwhile. In reality, the resource capability in all but the wealthiest of firms means that only a few such initiatives can be tackled at any one time. In considering strategic partnerships, we are concerned with the synergistic development of an old idea – that 2+2 can equal 5. It is intended that, in such a partnership, both sides will get more out than they put in. But more than this, the new competitive paradigm hinted at earlier requires that firms take a more innovative approach to business partnerships. Nevertheless, innovation alone is not enough: new forms of partnership need both innovation and structure to succeed.

Principles of true strategic partnerships

Successful partnerships between two firms must rest on principles as well as philosophy. The four principles on which true strategic partnerships must rest are trust, fairness, mutuality and wealth creation.

To try to create partnerships without believing in these four principles equates to accusing some customers or suppliers of having 'false partnership' aims. Partnerships founded on poor principles are unlikely to work as effectively, or last as long, as those built on more solid foundations.

A shared definition of what is meant by these principles will help in understanding them and translating them into powerful action plans.

Trust

Chambers defines trust as: 'worthiness of being relied on'. Other words like 'integrity', 'fidelity' and 'grounds for confidence' also spring to mind. Trust is the twin sister of confidentiality. It is formed slowly, but can quickly be ruined. And once ruined, it can take a long time to repair. Trust is created by actions rather than words alone. What people are seen to do, and equally not do, holds more powerful signals that what they say they will or will not do. Beginning the trust-building process depends on the firm doing something that encourages its customer to place trust in it. This can start a virtuous circle.

Fairness

To most people, fairness means dealing honestly with others, whether on a one-to-one or business-to-business basis. It evokes feelings of justice and reasonableness. Fairness in business does not always imply 50/50, it can mean 75/25 provided that both sides feel this is fair. An example of this would be where one partner has made a significantly greater contribution to the cost of something, and fairness should dictate that he or she receive the lion's share of the result. It could be said that a business deal is a good deal when it is fair and seen to be fair by both sides.

Mutuality

The notion of mutuality is close to fairness. It means an equitable sharing of benefits. Mutuality also means fairness in adversity. It is one thing to agree on what is mutually fair when benefits are to be split; quite another when costs have to be shared without any visible or tangible benefit being observed. Mutuality, therefore, is fairly shared costs and benefits. Mutual benefits will survive the ups and downs of business life, enduring over the long haul.

Wealth creation

'Wealth is created when the market value of the outputs exceeds the market value of the inputs.' So write Dobbins and Pike in *Capital Budgeting Techniques*. While this may sound a little simplistic at first, it captures all we need to know in defining what is meant by wealth creation. The 'inputs' here refer to the prime partnership assets described earlier, and the 'outputs' are the quantifiable benefits drawn from the partnership. Financial values can easily be attributed to most of these benefits.

True strategic partnerships are founded on these shared principles. Those who share them are more likely to be successful partners than those who do not. Many years ago, international consulting firm McKinsey & Co developed what became known as the '7 Ss'. The seven components referred to are:

- Structure
- Strategy
- Systems
- Skills
- Style
- Staff
- Shared values

McKinsey's proposed that, to be more successful, firms should concentrate on this list of items, but especially on the last. Its belief was that shared values among management and staff will, if properly applied, become the glue that holds the organization together and enables it to drive forward in harmony. Most people recognize the truth of this from their own experience. And if shared values are the glue bonding a single organization together, why should this not apply equally well to the bond between two organizations?

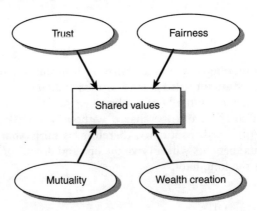

Figure 3.1 The role of shared values

True strategic partnership objectives

Firms are often said to be goal or objective driven, but it is better to be opportunity led. It is more appropriate to try to fit the objectives of the firm to the current and future opportunities it faces, rather than the other way round. Provided that the firm is sufficiently responsive to its environment, it should be able to shape its objectives to the opportunities it can see. In any case, this overcomes the difficulty once observed by Peter Drucker when commenting on objectives, that 'most firms don't know what their objectives are'.

Secondly, we are concerned with identifying and evaluating *future* opportunities, which may be different from today's opportunities. In some instances, future opportunities will be an extension of what already exists; in others, a thorough scan of future horizons will be necessary to pick out tomorrow's potential.

This approach is as true for the firm as a whole as it is for its partnership strategy, although the degree of vision is different. In searching for future corporate opportunities we must scan a much broader horizon. Economics, social policy, politics, demographics and the availability and cost of capital are among the matters central to strategic considerations at a corporate level. In partnership strategy the field of focus is much narrower, and is therefore relatively easier to manage. In seeking to create a partnership with another firm, we must examine the value chain formed by the customer, its suppliers (one of which will be us) and the customer's customer. Each of the firms downstream from us will need to be looked at, as will the interfaces between each. Scientific enquiry and artistic impression must combine in the right quantities to enable sound judgement of future opportunities.

None of this is to say that objectives are unimportant, simply that they should be placed after the identification of opportunities. Putting the horse before the cart, we can attempt to define the partnership opportunity, then decide its objectives. A written objective should be a statement of a future opportunity realized. Common sense says that it is easier to relate objectives to opportunities rather than the reverse.

People, projects and initiatives generally work better when clear, attainable and measurable objectives have been set. We can further divide partnership objectives into primary and secondary. This is not a measure of relative importance, but of magnitude. The primary objective of a strategic partnership is to create a sustainable, value-generating and enhancing platform on which to do business with specific major customers or suppliers. This means being able to create more value than would otherwise have been the case, rather than trying to divide what value already exists.

Five secondary objectives exist, stemming from the primary objective:

1 The firm aims to create and sustain a long-term relationship using more of its assets than the physical product or service and the account manager, in a way which is very difficult for competitors to copy.
2 The firm aims to become the favoured supplier among what is often a group of otherwise similar suppliers, and on a basis more enduring than lower prices.
3 Related to the first objective, the firm will be using the 'positive friction' which builds up in properly managed partnerships to search for new business opportunities.
4 Strategic partnerships have first-mover advantages: customers do not need two suppliers as partners in the same field.
5 Last, but certainly not least, the firm plans to realize its share of new value from each partnership. This value will be quantifiable in financial and other terms. These very specific objectives will be spelled out differently between firms and from one partnership initiative to another.

The overall context within which the creation of true strategic partnerships with selected customers and suppliers exists is to develop a new and better way of working together that becomes permanent. 'Better' means not only more profitable, but more rewarding in other ways as well.

The customer's perspective

This rationale may lead a supplier to the conclusion that strategic partnerships are one way of achieving superior performance and returns, but does not necessarily explain why a customer would want to enter into such a relationship. The first observation we can make in this respect is that not all customers will want to engage in a partnership of this type. Similarly, not all of a firm's customers will be suitable candidates. Some customers will take the view that they can continue as at present and that their needs are best served in this way. Others will not want a partnership because it necessitates giving up too much. These views are sometimes valid, but are sometimes based on inaccurate or incomplete information.

Put another way, there are some customers which will never be good partnership candidates because they do not believe in the underlying principles and philosophy of such an arrangement. Others may change their opinion over time as they acquire more knowledge of the subject. This will, to some extent, depend on the source of the information they receive, the channel through which it comes to them and the credibility of the supply partner. All of these matters can be influenced.

Assuming that a firm has more than one significant customer, removing from a list of 'possibles' those who fall into either of the above classifications will still leave some 'potentials'. By means of a more thorough analysis, some of these may be brought into focus as 'probables'. This issue will be addressed in Chapter 5. However, it is based on this final list of probables that we may proceed. But we are still faced with the original question: why would these customers want to enter into a closer relationship with a supplier? Several possibilities merit closer scrutiny, which may be viewed as being either defensive or offensive.

Defensive reasons

Inability to reach goals
The customer cannot see how strategic goals can be reached unless a radical change of some sort is made. Partnership with one or more key suppliers may offer a solution.

Lost knowhow
The customer has downsized the business, or plans to do so, and will lose people, knowhow and experience in the act. It might be possible to bridge the gap by striking up a new kind of relationship with a supplier able to offer the missing components.

Supply market situation
The customer is concerned by the supply situation. This may arise due to the relative strength of the supply market or because the customer sees a future situation in which supplies are scarce. A strategic relationship with a key supplier in these circumstances could be highly beneficial.

Reduction of prices
The customer believes that attracting certain suppliers into partnerships is a more effective way of obtaining lower prices. These are one-way, 'false partnerships' in which the supplier is asked to give more and take less. Partnerships aimed at lowering input costs fall into a different class. The distinction is subtle but important.

Affordability
The skills necessary to manage a specific set of actions do not exist within the customer's business, and forging a relationship is the only affordable way to gain access to them.

Offensive reasons

Market share drive
The customer plans to expand market share and needs the support of one or more important suppliers. The support called for may be financial, in the form of bigger discounts, knowledge based or founded on security of supply.

Exclusivity
New products and services often form an important part of any strategy. If a customer believes that one supplier in particular has a proven track record in this field, the customer may decide that the best way to lock the supplier into this strategy is to enter into a partnership that guarantees exclusivity, at least for a time. This has the simultaneous effect of locking the rest of the market out of these products or services, thus diminishing the supplier's scope.

Integration strategies
Some firms want to integrate more fully but cannot afford to make takeover bids for their suppliers. In other cases, because of regulatory limitations this may not be possible. Given a willing partner, an informal partnership can remove these obstacles.

Knowledge gaps
The customer wishes to expand in a particular direction and needs to acquire new knowledge or skills to do this. A partnership with a supplier possessing the necessary knowhow is one way to achieve this quickly.

Innovation gaps
Some customers recognize that innovation is one of the profit gateways to doing business in the twenty-first century. They also know that innovation resides not only in each firm in the value chain, but in the interfaces between firms. This thought process offers an opportunity to create new innovation possibilities and, through them, new wealth.

Customers are often conscious of a rationale for their seeking a partnership, but there are also instances where the reverse is true. In these cases, the wake-up call happens when a supplier comes along with a partnership proposition. Among the former group, customers can just as easily take the initiative in proposing a new arrangement, and this is the same as looking back down the value chain to the firm's own suppliers. There is a third group with several simultaneous reasons for wanting a partnership. Where these appear to be confused, it is important to attempt to clarify the customer's thinking before beginning the partnership. Starting from a basis of customer confusion about goals is likely to lead to a misinterpretation of actions or results.

Contracts

Once two or more partners have agreed to form a partnership, there are two possibilities in terms of how it will be regulated. One is to enter into a formal contract drawn up by lawyers, and the other is to do something less formal. This may range from an 'understanding' to an exchange of letters setting out the thrust of the partnership, though not necessarily the detail.

One point that should be made right away is that a legal contract will not save the partnership in the event of a serious dispute. The concept of the 'spirit of the contract' always exists, whether a legal document supports it or not. And once the spirit is broken, the end of the partnership is not far off.

In most cases, it is better not to have a legal document but to rely on something less formal. However, there are circumstances where a written contract is desirable. Firms finding themselves in this position may well find the following example contract of benefit. It illustrates a contract between a supplier of technical equipment in the defence industry, and applies to a customer in several geographic locations.

Example partnership contract

Introduction

The two parties to the contract will be Firm A, the supplier, and Firm B, the customer. The terms 'supplier' and 'customer' will be used throughout the contract to describe the partners. The overall purpose of the contract is to generate greater profitability for both partners by engaging in a series of business-building activities approved by both.

Conditions specific to the customer

1 Object of the contract

- Product commissioning.
- New product and process development.
- Service benefits.

2 Scope of supply (inclusions and exclusions)

- List of specified product components.
- Equipment.
- Spare parts.
- Monitoring by the supplier.
- Service, labour, repairs.
- Process engineering.
- Documentation.
- Training and other technical assistance.
- Technical specifications and detailed drawings not included.
- Language format English only.

3 Responsibilities of both parties

Supplier to be responsible for:

- undertaking surveys and analyses of current product;
- performance;
- production of reports with recommendations as to NPD;
- surveys and analyses of customer work practices at designated sites;
- costed evaluations with recommendations;
- commissioning trials;
- product and process handover;
- technical assistance and training.

Customer to be responsible for:

- providing all necessary assistance in technical and commercial studies;
- providing the supplier with financial and other performance data deemed necessary to carry out agreed studies;
- assisting with commissioning trials;
- provision of office accommodation and administrative support as required to complete studies.

4 Management of the contract

- Management steering group representing customer and supplier.
- SPI team to initiate and carry out the work.
- Meetings to be convened, reports, presentations on frequency to be agreed by steering group.

5 Financial conditions

- Equipment to be leased, lease with option to purchase, instalment contract.
- Residual value to be paid by customer at end of depreciated life.
- Financing of equipment purchase to be arranged by customer.
- Supplier prices quoted will be held for 90 days unless otherwise specified.
- Initial equipment prices established at the start of the contract will be held for 180 days from the date of contract.
- Initial prices for items other than equipment will be held for 90 days.
- At the end of the periods specified as being price firm, prices will be adjusted according to the agreed performance index.
- All prices exclude duties and taxes.
- Prices are quoted in US dollars, but from time to time can be paid in another currency chosen by common consent.
- Both parties have the right to renegotiate the contract, after 90 days have elapsed, in the case of hidden events or factors arising that were not established as part of the basis for the contract.
- Invoicing is based on equipment as it is delivered to the customer and consumable products as they are moved from the stocking site.
- An invoice will be produced on the last working day of each calendar month, specifying the amount of equipment and consumable products, plus any technical assistance or training outside the scope of the contract, and shall be paid in full by the customer within 14 (fourteen) days.
- In the event of a disputed invoice, the customer will, after detailing the basis of dispute, pay the remainder of the invoice on the date stipulated.
- Late payments will lead to interest of 1 per cent over the base lending rate as announced by the Bank of England, and shall be immediately due and payable.
- Customer is responsible for all additional expenses, including reasonable lawyers' fees incurred in collecting late payments.

6 Performance guarantee

- Cost savings in the first year of the contract, starting from the date of the contract, will be shared as follows: 70 per cent to the supplier, 30 per cent to the customer.
- In the second year of the contract, cost savings will be shared as follows: 55 per cent to the supplier, 45 per cent to the customer.
- In the third year, cost savings will be split 50/50.
- In subsequent years, cost savings will be split according to a formula agreed between the partners 90 days before the end of the third year.
- Costs incurred in setting up new programmes agreed by the partners will be shared on the same basis as cost savings, and for the three years of the contract.

7 Timeframe

■ The contract will be effective for an initial period of three years, with a renewal for two years if written notice is given 90 days in advance.
■ The 90 days' planning work needed to get the work programme ready will not form part of this contract.

8 Existing and future inventories

■ Inventories existing on the date of contract commencement, at any location, and forming part of the contract but not yet invoiced or paid for, will be taken into the contract on the terms specified herein.
■ Any technical assistance or training started before the date of the contract will be completed on the terms agreed.
■ Supplier will hold two weeks' consignment stock of equipment and three weeks' consignment stock of all consumable products.
■ In the event of poor financial condition, bankruptcy, reduction in production or cessation of production, the customer will indemnify the supplier for any inventory losses sustained for equipment or consumables held wholly on the customer's behalf.
■ The customer is responsible for providing secure, fenced areas where consignment stock is to be held.
■ The customer is responsible for moving equipment and consumable products, and for all unloading within customer locations.
■ The customer is responsible for insuring consignment inventory against damage or theft.
■ All equipment not forming part of the contract, but used in the contract, will remain the property of the supplier.

9 Definitions

■ Equipment, consumable products, technical assistance, training.
■ Delivery conditions.
■ Inventory, including consignment stocking.
■ Effective date, contract date.

10 Practices and technologies

■ In case of the customer changing manufacturing practice in a way that adversely affects the contract, the supplier will have the right to renegotiate the contract.
■ All trials shall be conducted by the SPI team, in which both partners will be represented at all times.
■ The supplier will be given all reasonable access to the customer's plant operations.

11 Taxes and duties

■ The customer will be liable for any taxes and duties that may be applied to the goods and services delivered under this contract.

12 Notices

■ All notices shall be effective if sent to the representatives designated by the customer and supplier.

13 Confidentiality

■ Everything that occurs within the contract shall be held to be confidential between the two partners, and will be released to a third party only with the written consent of both partners.
■ All public announcements, advertising or other publications relating to the contract shall be subject to verification and consent by both partners.

14 Developments and intellectual property rights

■ All developments relating to the equipment control systems are the property of the supplier.
■ During the contract, the customer shall have free licence to use goods over which the supplier has a patent.

15 Conflicts and strikes

■ In case of conflict or strike resulting in closure of the customer's plant, the contract duration will be extended by the length of the strike term, up to a total of 80 working days.
■ Plant closures of less than 80 continuous days will be regarded as temporary under the contract, while a continuous closure extending beyond 80 days will be considered permanent.
■ In the event of temporary plant closure by the customer, the contract will be suspended until the plant reopens.
■ If the parties to the contract decide to terminate the contract due to differences not resolvable by the steering group, written notice must be given.
■ In the event of a customer plant closure lasting longer than 80 working days, the supplier will have the option to terminate the contract.
■ In all cases of conflict or strike resulting in equipment or consumable materials being damaged or lost, the customer will be liable for payment for all materials manufactured specifically for the contract, plus any other reasonable costs incurred by the supplier as a direct result of the closure.
■ Payment of lost or damaged goods will be in full, minus any payments already made, and at the terms applying under the contract.

16 Patent defence

■ All patents held by both parties shall be fully protected during the duration of the contract.

17 Language

■ In case of translation of the contract, the English language version shall prevail.

18 Assignment

■ This contract will be binding on successors of the customer or supplier.

19 Arbitration

■ All disputes and disagreements over this contract shall be finally and exclusively settled by commercial arbitration.
■ The place and language of the arbitration will be chosen by common consent between the two parties to the contract.
■ The payment for such proceedings shall be shared equally between the partners.
■ The contract will be written in English law, which shall take precedence over all other law, irrespective of where disputes arise or arbitration takes place.

20 Liability

■ The customer shall assume all liabilities for production losses, however caused.
■ The customer shall assume all liabilities for damage to equipment or consumable products, except where these are being used in technical assistance training by the supplier.
■ The customer shall bear the cost of liability insurance for injury or death of supplier representatives engaged on partnership duties while on the customer's premises.

21 Termination of the contract

■ The customer or supplier may terminate the contract by mutual agreement, subject to written notice being given.
■ From and after the effective date of termination, neither partner shall have any further rights, privileges or obligations under this contract.

This draft partnership contract is intended as an example only. Firms wishing to enter into a partnership contract with their customers or suppliers should take expert legal advice before doing so.

Modelling strategic partnerships

The identification, creation and development of a customer or supplier into a strategic partner follow a path that can be modelled. This provides a framework into which the specific and unique variables and nuances that exist between two firms can be catered for. Partnership architecture must be sufficiently elastic to allow movement, but strong enough to sustain its mainly internal pressures. It is important to stress that the model shown in Figure 3.2 (page 50) is linear, not iterative. Progress is made by descending the steps in sequence until the bottom is reached, or by cutting off the process at one of the 'kill points'.

We can visualize the process as having two separate phases, ten distinct steps and three streams. The two phases are internal and joint, which means that the firm acting alone carries out some of the steps, while others are conducted jointly with the customer. For example, the second step, 'Define and shape an SPI' is done alone, but the third step, 'Gain first customer commitment', is done jointly. The ten steps can be seen on the model. The three streams referred to are headed the Activity stream, the Detail and the By whom stream.

In Chapters 4 to 10 we will conduct a step-by-step analysis of each part of the partnership process, beginning with its affordability. The aspects of partnership strategy which lay outside the model, but which are nonetheless crucial components in its make-up, will also be examined.

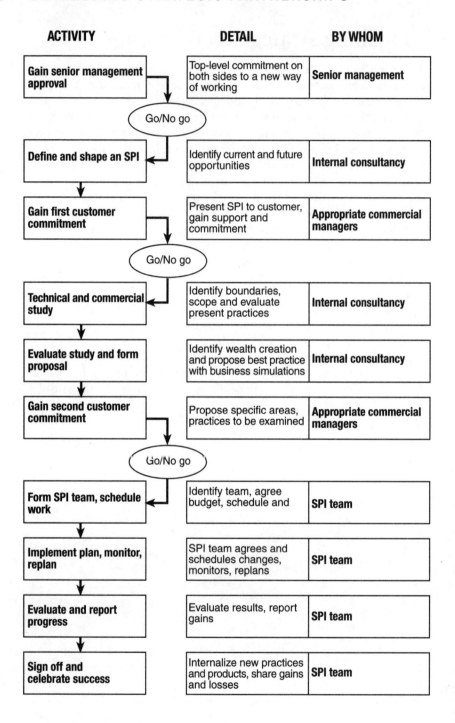

Figure 3.2 The strategic partnership model

Part II
Planning for a Strategic Alliance

Gaining internal approval

The first step in gaining approval for virtually anything in business is to be able to state how much it will cost and how much money it will make within a specific time. Subsequent steps depend on its affordability. So it is with gaining approval for approaching customers or suppliers with the offer of a strategic partnership. In addition, managers must be able to state what resources other than money will be needed if they are to gain internal approval for their plans. To develop our comprehension of the context in which the approval process takes place, we must first identify, and then examine, the several vital elements of business finance and resource management that apply. Understanding these more fully will set the scene for what follows as the partnership strategy unfolds.

Before embarking on a series of internal discussions about which customers or suppliers qualify as suitable partnership candidates, we must first decide whether a partnership strategy can be afforded. This means adopting one of the following policies:

1 Find new money with which to create partnerships.
2 Divert existing funds and resources.

It is a stark though far from simple choice. If the first option is chosen, an expense budget will have to be created from profits earned over a future period, or the firm will have to borrow money externally. There is a third way, to raise total costs as a means of paying for a partnership strategy. However, this will have an adverse impact on both margin and profit.

The second option is normally relatively simpler to take up, although it inevitably involves some difficult choices as well. There will always be people willing to fight their corner to maintain the resources they have worked hard to get. Yet if a partnership strategy is to be adopted the money must be found from somewhere, and this usually means raiding existing budgets.

As we saw in Chapter 1 when examining the concept and practice of degrees of strategic freedom, there are always expense accounts within the firm that will yield the required funds, the amount of which we shall look at shortly. It comes down to a question of willpower.

There are two parts to the cost involved in partnerships: setting up an expense budget and allocating the other resources needed to fire up and sustain the approach. Before analysing each in turn, we can look briefly at some important definitions.

A budget

A budget is a quantifiable financial statement setting out how particular objectives are to be met. It is therefore a statement of management intent. It sets out what management believes will happen in the firm during a future period. This time period may vary anywhere from a week to a year.

A budget is not a forecast, which is someone's opinion of what will happen, although it is probably based on one. Budgeting turns opinion into a specific and planned commitment concerning the allocation of resources. Clearly, then, budgeting is a forward-looking process.

A budget can only be as good as the managers who compile and monitor it against what actually happens, and take corrective action where necessary. It is an essential tool for decision making. Of course, no one can see into the future with 100 per cent accuracy, and the budgeting process recognizes this by utilizing the best management judgement available and committing the resulting numbers to paper.

Usually, the firm will prepare an overall master budget once a year, with total funds allocated to individual operating functions. These other budgets are used to monitor what is happening at a more local level once the period budgeted for begins. The firm's overall performance is measured against this master budget, while the performance of individual managers and their departments can be measured against their individual budgets. The same reasons that drive firms to create budgets for departments and product lines apply equally to partnership initiatives. And since budgeting is a way of life for most managers, there should be little difficulty in applying the principles to the partnership budgeting process.

In the case of partnership budgeting, the firm must decide where to charge the cost incurred. This will often be within either a marketing or sales department's budget in the case of customers, or to the buying department in the case of suppliers. Another option is to establish a separate budget, which in some cases may also be a profit centre.

Since managers are often forced to start the budgeting process without statistical knowledge or experience of previous partnerships – there has to be a first time for everyone – applying the principles of zero-based budgeting is a good approach. The best advice on this topic as it applies to partnerships is to try to work with the grain, that is, to use existing systems and methodologies as far as possible.

The budgeting process

When viewed at a firm-wide level, the process usually begins with a sales forecast. This is an expression by sales managers of what they expect to happen over the following year. It is the key step, because expense budgets will eventually be based on the sales forecast. Sales managers are noted for their optimism when future business is being discussed in general terms; and for their pessimism when it comes to forecasting that business in detail. Like everyone else in the firm, they do not have a crystal ball. Forecasting is a risky business, but there are ways to reduce the risks involved. One approach involves the following seven-step method:

1 *Analyse the market.* What has changed or seems likely to change? Have any competitors left or entered the market? Are there any socioeconomic, political, technological or demographic factors that will affect the markets in which the firm operates? Are customers' needs changing? In cases where the firm has a number of important customers, managers will need to consider each of them in turn, producing a forecast for each. The latest market research statistics, sales managers' detailed knowledge and the most up-to-date internal statistics will all help.

2 *Analyse the product or service.* Is it still in demand? Is that demand rising or falling? What about demand for competitors' products? Does what is offered need to be altered in some way?

3 *Build and check assumptions.* From the above analysis, it should be possible to list the main assumptions for next year. These will appear as a set of bullet points, preferably on no more than one or two pages. These assumptions should then be checked by referring them to other people with a knowledge of the markets in which the firm is positioned. Such people might include any sister firms in the group, consultants, market analysts, key suppliers, and recently retired people with a specialist knowledge of the marketplace.

4 *Select the appropriate forecasting technique.* Apply this technique to the assumptions made to see what numbers are produced. It is often desirable to use two or even three techniques so as to be able to make comparisons.

5 *Adjust the forecast.* This may be done by applying a checklist of relevant questions.

6 *Solicit expert opinion.* Sales managers are not the only people in the firm with expert knowledge and, in any case, they may have overlooked, overstated or understated some factor that it is easier for others to spot. This step goes hand in hand with the one above.

7 *Check the forecast against the firm's objectives.* This is often where the process becomes bogged down, because senior management may have expressed aims for the business that are not supported by the sales forecast. In such cases, something has to give or managers will spend much of the coming year telling lies or making excuses about what is happening. A key question to ask is: what is realistic in the circumstances?

This method is not guaranteed to produce the right answers every time, but a scientific system creates an audit trail that can be analysed when variances occur. At the same time, managers can replicate the process more easily from one budget period to another, hopefully increasing accuracy over time. Another advantage is that this method produces a relatively simple table, an example of which is shown below.

Table 4.1 Customer X sales forecast

Latest year's sales of product A	20 000 units
Next year's demand	+ 5%
Next year's change due to competition	No change
Next year's change due to relative price	– 1%
Next year's change due to promotion	+ 2%
Next year's change due to economic factors	– 2%
Next year's change due to demographics	+ 1%
Next year's change due to product lifecycle curve	– 3%
Next year's change due to new technology introduced	+ 6%
Overall effect:	<u>21 580</u>

	£	Year-on-year change
Latest year's income	250 000	210 000
Less variable costs	90 000	78 000
Gross contribution	160 000	132 000
Less fixed cost allocation	75 000	75 000
Net contribution	85 000	57 000
Next year's income	300 000	
Less variable costs	105 000	
Gross contribution	195 000	
Less fixed cost allocation	75 000	
Net contribution	120 000	

On one table, we are attempting to show the following:

1 Latest year's sales volume and value.
2 Next year's demand factors and the planned result of these on volume.
3 Latest year's and next year's contribution levels.

Back-up sheets would add detail as necessary. For example, the sales manager responsible for this customer might want to see a more detailed description of both variable and fixed costs.

Whether this methodology or another is preferred, it should have the capability of being transferred from its overall sales budgeting context to an individual customer or supplier.

Budgeting rules

Every budget is a bargain
A budget is the result of pull and push between managers in the firm. What top management wants and what others believe is possible do not always amount to the same thing. Usually when this happens, top management's expectations are the higher of the two. A process of negotiation follows, at the end of which a bargain is struck which satisfies top management and to which other managers are genuinely committed.

The budget is a control tool
Once the various budgets have been agreed with those involved, it is good practice to use the budget as a control tool when the action starts. The most commonly used method for this is variance analysis. A variance is the difference between what was planned to happen and what actually occurred.

Variances can be either positive or negative. Managers should avoid wasting too much time examining each one, but should concentrate their mental energy on those variances that begin to show a trend and those that are clearly significant in nature. Having discovered a significant variance, the cause must be searched for. Check with colleagues to see if they have similar variances. A production variance caused by a machine failure will affect everywhere else in the business – and everyone else's budgets.

Get the data fast
The critical element in monitoring performance is getting the data fast. There is little point in knowing that the January budget was overspent by 20 per cent if the information is not available until March. The same applies to managing others with budget responsibility.

Fast data aids quick decisions
Accountants can draw a manager's attention to budget variances, but then it is up to the manager to do something about it. Corrective action, when necessary, often requires a quick decision, frequently involving others. Get the decision made as soon as possible and don't forget to tell the people who need to know the new plan.

A budget is a commitment
If too much flexibility is allowed then that commitment can wane. On the other hand, there is no point in remaining committed to a budget that is clearly no longer attainable, perhaps for reasons outside the manager's control. A middle way is to stick to the original budget but produce a periodic 'latest forecast'. The original budget stays in place and managers produce a new forecast every month or quarter. Actual performance is then measured against both.

Zero-based budgeting

The type of budgeting normally applied in firms – incremental budgeting – has the advantage of simplicity, but the disadvantage that errors made in previous years tend to get carried forward from one budget to another. This is because managers rarely question budget holders in sufficient depth about every aspect of their budget. This weakness is especially true of cost budgeting.

Zero-based budgeting uses a different method. It takes no account of any previous levels of activity and applies a far more critical approach, starting from scratch. It is time consuming, but offers the benefit of focusing managers' attention on the activities that are most likely to produce the right results in terms of the firm's overall aims and needs.

There are five discrete steps involved in zero-based budgeting:

1 Senior management will produce a set of assumptions about the economic situation as a whole. These assumptions will be fleshed out as the process goes down the line to make them more relevant to specific centres of activity within the firm.
2 Step two is to identify 'decision units'. These may be cost centres, profit centres, investment centres or budget centres.
3 The third step is, in practice, four separate actions. First, the manager concerned lays out the decision unit objectives, following discussions with superiors and subordinates. Secondly, the current activities and the resources employed are described in sufficient detail for a more senior manager to understand. Thirdly, alternative ways of achieving the stated objectives are discussed, with the best one being selected. And fourthly, the decision unit manager describes different levels of possible activity and the resources required to generate them. These are often described in three or four activity and resource-level stages.
4 The decision unit manager now ranks these options according to their fit with the overall business goals and available funding, placing the options most likely to achieve them at the top. In cases where the decision unit manager believes that a higher level of funding will pro-

duce better results, he or she will be expected to present the argument in detail.

5 Senior management can now evaluate all the packages from the various decision units, selecting those most likely to achieve corporate goals. Conventional budgets may now be prepared, although of course most of the work has already been done.

As previously stated, zero-based budgeting is time consuming. It is not recommended that firms adopt the process for every decision centre, or necessarily every year. However, there are certain conditions in which it can be highly valuable:

- where the firm is 'stuck' in the budgeting process and cannot find the best fit between activity levels and resources;
- where resources need to be sharply reduced, but activity levels less so;
- where senior management wishes to introduce greater responsibility and authority at decision-unit level;
- where more data is needed than is normally produced using the traditional, incremental approach;
- where more creativity is required;
- where a new business unit is being established.

Partnership strategy comes under the last bullet, in a cost budgeting sense. Zero-based budgeting is ideal as a method of thinking about the allocation of existing costs and how they might relate to a new partnership venture. The technique should first be applied, rigorously, to the firm's really significant cost headings. It inevitably generates savings that are then reallocated to the development of the firm's partnership strategy.

Capital project appraisal

Opportunities and resources

Two things are certain in almost every business: there are always plenty of opportunities for the firm to spend its capital, and at the same time these capital resources are always scarce. There never quite seems to be enough money available to fund all the strategies that managers would like to undertake. Given this situation, choices must be made regarding the allocation of capital to various projects. Almost invariably, this means weighing up the benefits of competing projects, of which a partnership is one among many. As well as making an outstanding marketing case for a partnership initiative, managers must make an equally cogent argument using hard financial numbers.

There are three principal methods of doing this:

■ payback;
■ return on investment;
■ discounted cashflow.

Payback

The concept of payback is straightforward. The manager relates the additional cash resulting from the completion of a project to the cost of doing it, and then works out how long it will take to recover the latter from the former. For example, if the firm spends £10 000 on a project that results in its gaining an additional £2000 in cash, the payback period will be five years (10 000 divided by 2000).

When everything else is considered equal, a firm will choose the project with the shortest payback from among all the projects competing for its capital. We can see how this operates from the further example below.

A firm employs three administrative staff and a supervisor. Everything is done manually, with the following annual costs:

	£
3 olorko at £10 000 oach	30 000
1 accounts supervisor at £15 000	15 000
Stationery and other costs	5 000
Total departmental costs	50 000

The firm is considering the purchase of a small computer that will have an estimated economic life of five years and will enable it to reduce the number of staff employed. The annual cost of the new department is estimated as follows:

	£
1 computer operator at £14 000	14 000
1 part-time assistant at £7000	7 000
1 supervisor at £16 000	16 000
Other costs:	
Depreciation	4 000
Computer stationery and maintenance	3 000
Total departmental costs	44 000

Since depreciation is a non-cash cost, the cash outflow resulting from the change would be £40 000 and the annual estimated cash savings £10 000 each year. The payback period is therefore the cost of the computer at £20 000, divided by the annual cash savings of £10 000, which is 2 years. The payback sum can be expressed as:

$$\frac{£20\ 000}{£10\ 000} = 2\ \text{years}$$

Return on investment

This calculates the relationship between the cost of the project and the resulting net profit. The sum can be expressed as:

$$\frac{\text{Average net profit}}{\text{Average cost of the project}} \times 100 = \text{ROI}$$

Average net profit is the average net profit of the firm over a given number of years, and is easily found by dividing the total of the former by the latter.

Average cost of the project needs a little more explanation. When the firm invests in, say, more manufacturing plant, the cost is depreciated each year and charged to the profit and loss account. If a machine is purchased for £20 000 and the straight-line method of deprecation over four years is used, then the firm will recover £5000 a year until the machine is written off four years later. For the purpose of calculating return on investment (ROI), begin with the initial investment and divide it by two. In this case, the average project cost is £10 000.

We can see how ROI works by considering two projects competing for the firm's capital resources (see Table 4.2). We will assume that both projects have an initial capital cost of £80 000 and an economic life of six years.

ROI is easy to apply and has the correct focus – on profit. However, it does ignore the time value of money. Although Project B generates a slightly higher ROI, most of the profits come at the back end of the project, and we are assuming that £1 invested now has the same value when it is returned in five or six years from now. Obviously, this is untrue.

Table 4.2 Return on investment (ROI)

	Project A	Project B
Average project cost	£40 000	£40 000
	£	£
Resulting profits:		
Year 1	22 000	5 000
Year 2	15 000	5 000
Year 3	9 000	8 000
Year 4	8 000	10 000
Year 5	4 000	16 000
Year 6	2 000	18 000
	60 000	62 000
Average net profit	10 000	10 333
Return on investment	25.0%	25.8%

Discounted cashflow

The third method is discounted cashflow (DCF), which does iron out the problem of the time value of money referred to earlier. Everyone understands that money has a different value in the future and Table 4.3 shows why this is the case.

Suppose that £100 is invested with the bank now at an investment rate of 10 per cent. What will happen to the money in the future?

Table 4.3 Discounted cashflow (DCF)

1 year later	£110.00
2 years later	£121.00
3 years later	£133.10
4 years later	£146.40
5 years later	£161.10
and so on...	

If the £100 can be invested at 10 per cent, then it makes no difference whether it returns £100 now or £161.10 in five years' time (cash calls excepted and ignoring both inflation and risk).

There are two ways in which DCF can be applied, techniques known as net present value (NPV) and internal rate of return (IRR). We can briefly examine both here. For a more detailed explanation, see *Management Accounting for Marketing and Business* by Richard Kotas.

Net present value

To use NPV, a particular rate of interest must be applied to discount all future cashflows so as to arrive at their present-day values. The excess of the discounted total over the cost of the project is its NPV. The higher the NPV, the more attractive the project.

This is how it works: we will assume that two projects are being considered, each involving a capital cost of £40 000, each with an estimated economic life of six years. We will also assume an interest rate of 10 per cent to compile the NPV table shown as Table 4.4.

Table 4.4 Net present value (NPV)

| | Conversion | Project A | | Project B | |
		Net cashflow	Present value	Net cashflow	Present value factor
Year 1	0.909	21 000	19 890	5 000	4 545
Year 2	0.826	16 000	13 216	6 000	4 956
Year 3	0.751	9 000	6 759	8 000	6 080
Year 4	0.683	8 000	5 464	10 000	6 830
Year 5	0.621	4 000	2 484	16 000	9 936
Year 6	0.564	2 000	1 128	18 000	10 152
		60 000	48 140	63 000	42 427
Less cost of project			40 000		40 000
Net present value			8 140		2 427

Even though Project B generates a higher net cashflow, Project A will be preferred because it produces more net cash at the beginning of the project.

Internal rate of return

The use of IRR discounts future net cashflows by applying a particular interest rate against them until the sum of the discounted cashflows equals the cost of the project. In the example in Table 4.5, the firm is considering a project costing £96 280 and having an expected life of 6 years. In finding the right IRR, we proceed by trial and error. We will begin by using 8 per cent as the hurdle rate.

Table 4.5 Internal rate of return (IRR)

	Net cashflow	Conversion factor	Present value
Year 1	42 000	0.926	38 892
Year 2	32 000	0.857	27 424
Year 3	18 000	0.794	14 292
Year 4	16 000	0.735	11 760
Year 5	8 000	0.681	5 448
Year 6	4 000	0.630	2 520
	120 000		100 336

The present value of £100 336 is more than the cost of the project and therefore we have used too low an IRR. A second attempt will use 10 per cent (Table 4.6).

Table 4.6 Internal rate of return (IRR)

	Net cashflow	Conversion factor	Present value
Year 1	42 000	0.909	38 178
Year 2	32 000	0.826	26 432
Year 3	18 000	0.751	13 518
Year 4	16 000	0.683	10 928
Year 5	8 000	0.621	4 968
Year 6	4 000	0.564	2 256
	120 000		96 280

The discounted total is now equal to the cost of the project at £96 280, and so the IRR is 10%.

The significance of NPV and IRR
The NPV of £8140 in the example referred to as Project A in Table 4.4 is the profit made on the project. If the £40 000 needed to finance the project was borrowed at 10 per cent, then £8140 represents the net gain after loan repayments and interest charges on the reducing balance.

The IRR in the second example is 10 per cent. Had the £96 280 needed for the project been borrowed at this rate, the gain on the project would have been nil. If, however, it had been borrowed at 7 per cent, then there would have been a gain of 3 per cent on the project's capital.

Therefore, where the IRR is in excess of the cost of the capital, the project appears worthwhile.

DCF is concerned with cashflows and not profit or loss. Depreciation should not be taken into account, therefore, because this is a charge against profit, not cash. It is also important to remember that any tax liabilities will affect cashflows, depending on the timing of payments. When using NPV, the rate of interest must be applied that accurately reflects the cost of capital to the firm. Projects are often financed by internally generated capital; in such cases, it is essential to calculate the true cost of that capital having regard to the sources of capital, either share or loan capital.

When considering partnerships from a financial viewpoint, two concepts are of vital interest, profit and cashflow. The techniques described in this section are widely used to calculate both. They can be used not only to calculate the profit or cashflow resulting from different types of project, including partnerships, but also to verify possible tactics within a partnership once it has begun.

The discussion also triggers off another issue: whether a finance expert should be part of the partnership team approach. We will return to this question in Chapter 9. In the meantime, we should consider what other resources must be marshalled in order to mount a successful partnership campaign.

Other resources

In practice, all resources boil down to finance. However, for the purpose of our discussion here, we will divide the resources needed into the three other groups of people, skills and materials. All three have a financial cost and value, and all are wrapped in the partnership envelope.

Each partnership will be different in a variety of ways, so it is impossible to be specific on the skill set required to set up and operate a particular partnership. What is possible, however, is to offer some general guidelines that can be tailored to meet a specific set of circumstances. These may be discussed briefly here, but will be explored in considerably greater depth in Chapter 9.

People

As the process develops, a team will be created. A team should have a leader. In the majority of cases, the team leader will report to the manager with overall responsibility for the partnership.

There will be a core team comprising members who devote a significant portion of work time to the initiative, and a number of satellite members who are co-opted as the need arises. The team can be seen as a set of competencies brought together to manage a partnership and drive it forward to meet its objectives.

Skills

Two types of skills are needed to manage or work in a partnership: team effectiveness skills and functional skills. Both must exist in sufficient measure to achieve close working relationships and more quantifiable objectives. Among others, team effectiveness skills will include communication and conflict resolution. Examples of functional skills are financial or logistics management.

Materials

The single most important material component that the team needs is a place to meet. Once this has been agreed, further materials, such as computer hardware and software, can be organized. Other material elements may range anywhere from physical product to be used in trials to literature needed to carry the message around the two firms.

Money

Although in practice finance will be addressed at the same time as the other elements, perhaps before some of them, it also ends the process of assembling the various pieces of the partnership puzzle. The amount of money needed to start a partnership, as well as the amount required to sustain it, will form a cost budget. The other half of the equation is the income which it is hoped will be derived from the partnership. These two statements form the financial plan as well as becoming the basis of the plan as a whole.

As we will see, however, the budget cannot yet be completed. This is because each partnership is different and the precise ways in which funds will be allocated, and the specific initiatives to which they and other resources will ultimately be allocated, have not yet been determined by discussion with the partner.

What now remains is to put the pieces together into a sound, reasoned argument as to why the firm should choose to create funds, or more likely divert funds from one part of the enterprise to another. The reality, of course, is that the work necessary to bring the firm to this state of readiness is unlikely to have taken place without the approval, or at least knowledge, of senior management. Someone at the top of the firm has therefore been ready to listen to the partnership story with an open mind. In many instances, it goes far beyond this. Managers are already committed to trying this approach with one or more customers or suppliers and what has taken place so far is part of a feasibility study.

Nevertheless, managers preparing for internal approval should take nothing for granted. All the underlying principles of persuasive argument should be used to turn ideas into action. These principles and the appropriate tools will be discussed more fully in Chapter 8.

What is being sought is a decision, in principle, to commit resources to a new strategy. Unlike most other strategies the firm adopts, however, this one depends entirely on there being a willing partner; willing, that is, to make an equal commitment. A tango with only one dancer is not really a tango. The stage has not yet been reached when the firm knows whether partnership suspects can be turned into prospects, and so the decision can be in principle only. The plan advances the total process a little further than this, however, because once the decision has been made to progress to the next step, much of the groundwork will already be in place.

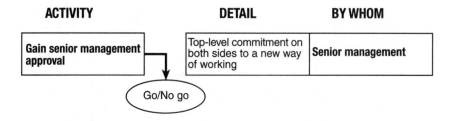

Figure 4.1 The strategic partnership model excerpt

As the model in Figure 4.1 demonstrates, there is a kill point here. In other words, there may be a change of heart on the part of senior management between commissioning the study and hearing the argument spelled out in detail. This can occur for a variety of reasons. The firm could experience a crisis of some sort between the two events, circumstances might change radically in another way, there might be an alteration in the composition of board members, or top management could simply change its collective mind about wanting to develop the concept of strategic partnerships. In all of these cases the result is the same: the strategy is killed on the drawing board.

The assumption here, though, is that this is not the case. We must proceed on the basis that board approval is gained and that the team can now progress to the next step. In fact there are two steps, one of which is hidden in the section of the model displayed above, the other being the subsequent linear step of identifying, profiling and selecting partners.

Contained within the overall strategy of partnerships is the notion that to be truly successful in long-term relationships, suppliers must shift the emphasis from being makers and sellers to being consultants; not instead, but as well as. It is a question of balance. The rationale for this is clear: customers perceive most supplying firms in a particular cluster as being similar or even identical. Whatever changes the supplier makes to the way in which it approaches its customers and does business with them, it remains a maker and seller of goods and services.

Many customers see supplier changes as 'just another angle to sell more'. Often they are right and, when they are, it is because the supplier's methodology is not authentic. 'Selling more' usually means someone else selling less. Relative market share may change, at least for a time, but the market remains the size it was before the action took place. The common response of competitors is to find another way to sell more, thus taking back any lost market share, though not necessarily from the firm which gained it last time around. Customers watch this process with a sense of mildly amused detachment. It affects their suppliers, but has little long-term impact on anything else.

Consultants come from the same stable; they want to sell more too. Customers realize this when they hire them, but usually believe that the value of what they are getting is greater than its cost. While this is true of the goods purchased from their suppliers, the supplier is seen as partial, the consultant impartial. When they hire a consultant, most firms believe that they help create new wealth or, at a minimum, will add value to the business. And in any case, consultants can be hired and fired at will, something that is rarely true of suppliers. All these points are relevant, but the issue of impartiality is the most important. Shifting the emphasis from being a maker-seller to being a maker-seller-consultant can achieve supplier distinction by building credibility.

Saying it is one thing, however – doing it in a way that is believable and credible to customers is another. It is difficult to demonstrate your credibility unless there is a sustained opportunity in the proper environment. A strategic partnership is just such a place. And the partnership process begins when top management approval is given. This is the right time for those tasked with establishing the partnership strategy in the firm to add 'consultant' to maker-seller, and to start thinking more objectively about the creation of new wealth and adding genuine value to supplier–customer relationships. This done, we can now move on to the next stage in the model (Figure 4.2).

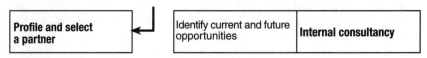

Figure 4.2 The strategic partnership model excerpt

Profiling and selecting a partner

Now that internal board-level approval has been gained, the central question facing the firm is how to choose which of its customers or suppliers to approach first. There are two risks attached to the ultimate decision: rejection by the prospect and the attitude of other customers if they discover that they were not first.

In practice, the first risk is the lesser of the two. If the prospect rejects the offer of a partnership, it will be for one of the following four reasons:

1 The customer does not see the advantages or benefits in a partnership that the firm previously believed would arise. In other words, the firm over- or underestimated the customer's response.
2 The customer does see the benefits inherent in a partnership, but not with this particular supplier.
3 The customer is unsure. This may simply mean that it needs to weigh up the proposal. It could also signal that the firm must sharpen its presentation or its argument, or both, in future.
4 The wrong customer was selected by the firm. In this case, any of the three reasons above may apply, or it may mean that the selection criteria used by the firm are wrong.

The outcome of rejection, whatever the reason, will be to lessen the firm's confidence in its ability to turn some customers or suppliers into true strategic partners, making it slightly harder next time. This usually only becomes a significant factor if several rejections occur. At the same time, the customer rejecting the offer is alerted to the fact that the supplier is seeking a different kind of relationship with some customers. However, it is difficult to see how this might disadvantage the supplier in future dealings with that customer, since the customer was approached with a view to being involved. And finally, rejection pushes up the cost of partnerships, due to the sunk cost of developing a proposal for the customer making the rejection.

The second risk, that of other customers demanding to know why they were not first, is potentially trickier, but only at a peripheral level. We are assuming first that other customers will learn about the new strategy from a source other than the firm making the proposal, and secondly that this infers there is anything to be defensive about.

Quite the contrary is true: it opens up a dialogue on the subject, which if handled properly saves a great deal of time and effort.

The proper response will depend first on whether a new partnership has been started which soaks up the firm's resources, and secondly on whether the customer is high on its list of partnership candidates. If the proposing firm's resources do not stretch to a second partnership being considered at present, the discussion should centre on when would be the appropriate time. In the second instance, the firm must make a decision on whether to move the customer to the top of its list and open discussions right away, or to postpone discussions to a later date. The most sensible answer the firm has to the question of 'why not us?' is that to undertake a partnership initiative without the necessary resources being in place on both sides is to heighten the risk of failure, or at least lessen the chance of success. This has the added virtue of being true.

Managing the second risk also means deciding whether to 'go public' with the strategy. Making a public announcement has the advantages of apparent openness and lower costs in explaining the strategy to a group of other firms, but these are outweighed by the disadvantages. Crucial among these is setting up expectations among a group of customers or suppliers for something which, by implication, they are likely to believe is imminent. The firm will almost certainly be unable to manage these expectations in the short term, and in the longer term most customers will have forgotten the original announcement, thus making it redundant. Secondly, a core element of partnership strategy is that each partnership is unique. The dynamics that are created between a supplier and one of its customers do not necessarily exist between the same supplier and a different customer. To inform an entire industry about partnership strategy in one hit implies that the firm has, or can formulate, a proposal for everyone in that industry. This is unlikely to be true.

The correct method, therefore, is to identify prospects and approach them one at a time, formulating a unique partnership proposal for each one. The first part of this process will be made a little simpler by using a system of profiling filters that enable managers to examine several candidates at once, narrowing the field in a series of progressive steps. It is the identification of these filters and the sequence in which they are used that will be the focus of this chapter.

To begin the discussion, however, we will concentrate briefly on a different aspect of partnership selection policy. While it is true that every selection procedure contains some element of subjectivity – indeed, subjectivity is beneficial in this case – there is a real danger of allowing this to take over in decision making.

Every sales manager has favourite customers and every buyer has favourite suppliers. What makes them favourite is a complex set of factors, partly quantitative and partly qualitative. When these factors are summarized in decision making, it can lead to the conclusion that the favourite is the best. This might be a long way from the truth. Favourite may mean nothing more than that the firm gets a favourable hearing, which is not the right basis for approaching possible partners. A more scientific method must be used for selecting partners. In any event, it will be possible to get a favourable hearing without relying on favourites. Of course, there will be occasions when the two factors tally: when a favourite customer or supplier is selected on the basis of more thoughtful criteria.

Selection filters

A discussion of the criteria to be used when profiling and selecting partners may begin with drawing up a list of filters. Having reviewed this list, we can proceed to arrange it in a way that creates a successively finer set of instruments through which to pass possible partnership candidates. At the end of this screening process, a short list of candidates will remain, and personal judgement must then be used to make the final choice.

Although they are not arranged in any particular order for the moment, the filters we will use are the following.

Financial

The customer must be able to provide the firm with, say, £1 million in additional sales revenue. Alternatively or simultaneously, the firm must be able to generate an additional contribution of £250 000. The timeframe for these achievements is the first year. Subsequent years will carry additional revenues and contributions, yet to be determined. The figures given here are merely meant to be illustrative.

Share

The initiative must create the opportunity to build the customer's market share and, simultaneously, the firm's share of the customer's market. There may be sound additional reasons for this objective, related to offensive or defensive generic strategy, the building of competitive entry barriers or customer or supplier exit barriers.

Stability

Partners must be stable; especially, but not exclusively, in a financial sense. It is pointless to develop a costly partnership strategy with a firm which cannot afford to pull its weight or, worse, which fails before the partnership rewards can be fully realized because of unstable management.

Education

There are at least two aspects to consider here: the level of general educational standards in the market as a whole, and the educational standards of the management and workforce. Poor standards in either case will inhibit the scope of a partnership initiative as well as the partner's ability to translate ideas into action. Another feature of this filter is that a large disparity of educational standards between partners can cause negative friction as well as slowing progress.

Culture

If we compare the culture in China with that in the USA, we will observe marked differences in outlook. This is often also true of close geographic neighbours. Similarly, firms can co-exist in the same industry yet hold notably disparate views on how the industry works. These differences can exist for many reasons, one of which is cultural.

Technology

There are clearly observable gaps in technology between the former communist countries in eastern Europe and the more technologically developed nations in western Europe. One twist to this is that firms in eastern Europe need strategic partners from the west because they need to move rapidly up learning curves. Partnerships can be an excellent way of obtaining knowhow at relatively low cost. Potential obsolescence is a slightly different angle on this issue, used here in relation to equipment.

Respect

Mutual respect is far more valuable than like or dislike. Ideally, the firm wants to work with suppliers and customers which it respects and likes and with which these feelings are mutual. However, in the marathon to build both, respect should take precedence. Respect is a keystone of trust, a vital ingredient in successful partnerships.

Problems

All firms have problems, some severe, others not so. Some seem intractable. With delicate handling, a problem can be a gateway to a partnership. However, the firm must avoid giving the impression that it necessarily knows the answer; few serious problems are that simple. Also, the payoff of solving the problem must be worth the cost, the risk of failure and the effort involved.

Open mind

People in some firms appear to have closed minds, while others seem willing to consider new ideas and practices. Where this counts is at top management level, since this is where the entry to a successful partnership is made.

Alliances

An alliance between two firms, one of which is a customer or supplier, can open the way to a partnership. The obvious way in which this happens is when an alliance is created and one party is already a partner with the supplier. This creates an opportunity for an extended partnership.

Management

Opportunities exist for partnerships where the prospect would like to embark on a particular course of action, but is prevented or inhibited from doing so due to the inability of its management to see it through. This can stem from the poor calibre of management or the existence of a specific knowhow gap.

Chemistry

Some people get on well together and others do not. Often, one or both parties involved in a commercial relationship are heard to say that there is good 'chemistry'. Few people can quantify this precisely, but everyone knows what it means. There is also a set of emotional responses that appear to sit comfortably with the feeling of good chemistry, while the reverse is true of relationships which feel awkward. The same is true in relationships between firms.

Therefore, the 12 variables we must consider when profiling and selecting partners are:

1   Financial
2   Share
3   Stability
4   Education
5   Culture
6   Technology
7   Respect
8   Problems
9   Open-mindedness
10 Alliances
11 Management
12 Chemistry

Focusing on the bigger picture for a moment, the reason for the strategic partnership approach being applied should warrant another look:

1 Gain more future sales and profit than would otherwise have been the case.
2 Get back the original investment as quickly as possible.
3 Create a broader base with the customer, using more of the firm's assets.
4 Gain the strategic high ground and shut out competitors.

Since we are trying to form new business partnerships for strategic reasons, and most firms exist to make a profit, it seems sensible to begin by considering financial criteria as the first filter.

The first filter

The first screening question then becomes: given the cost of the investment, can this customer give us £1 million in extra sales and/or £250 000 in additional contribution? In the case where a partnership with a supplier is being considered, the question becomes: given the cost of the investment, can this supplier help us gain £1 million in greater efficiencies and/or another £250 000 in contribution?

There are two factors to bear in mind in trying to form an answer to the question: the extent to which the additional revenue and contribution can come from existing wealth; and the amount of new wealth that must be created for the objective to be realized.

Put another way, the consideration is whether the firm can get what it wants from business it already knows about, or whether it also has to tap into potential. The latter will depend on such factors as demand elasticity in the customer's product-markets and how well equipped the customer is to take advantage of any latent demand. Therefore, in trying to make this calculation, the supplier is forced to make an assessment of the customer's degree of strategic freedom. In the act of making this assessment, the firm moves from its original seller-maker position towards seller-maker-consultant.

Every supplier knows that it is much easier to calculate the value of existing business, whether it currently has that business or not, than to evaluate the value of some future business, which by its very nature is shrouded in uncertainty. An analogy would be that it is relatively simple for a supplier of sports shoes to calculate the amount of existing potential. The supplier begins by knowing or finding out the size of the volume in a given retail market and deducting the volume it currently supplies to that market. The difference is the theoretical potential. The potential will never be realized, of course, because in acting, the supplier is forced to push against existing competitors who together make up the difference. The relative strengths of these competitors will heavily influence the competitive outcome. Alternatively, the supplier can look at its individual retail customers and perform the same calculation.

What is rather more difficult to evaluate is the effect that television and Internet shopping will have on the market for sports shoes. One issue of concern is whether these new channels will increase the market size overall, or if they will simply cannibalize existing channels. If it is believed that they will help increase total volume, how much of that new volume will be gained by an individual retailer and how much by individual suppliers?

So we have two parts to the equation. The first part is concerned with how much of the existing theoretical potential the firm can gain without triggering off a competitive response, and the second relates to how the market will be shaped by new forces.

It would be very difficult for any sports shoe manufacturer to evaluate these matters on its own, if only because there is limited access to the data that exist. The retailer has access to different data, mainly derived from checkout scanning systems; if these two sets of data are added together, 2+2 can equal 5. It is not merely a matter of data, of course, valuable though this can be in the right hands. Interpretation is the critical issue, and there is a better chance of having an agreed interpretation when the analysis is done between sports shoe manufacturer and retailer than when it is done by either side alone. This holds true for any other potential set of partners in any other industry. The process of comparing interpretive analyses with a partner leads almost inevitably to new insights.

However, we have moved on a step too far. We must first discuss how the financial criteria should be applied to seeking a partnership that does not yet exist, when the opportunity to share and explore understanding with another firm is still merely a hope. The firm's resource commitment must be made before this aspect of a partnership can be realized. However, in some cases, a sufficiently strong relationship between seller and buyer will already be in place which will enable the supplier to explore these questions at an informal level. If and when a partnership materializes with this customer, the process can be cemented in place as part of the way they work together.

For the present, however, there may be no alternative but to apply the knowledge that exists in the firm alone, without the ability to gain a second input. It is on this assumption, the worst-case scenario, that we will proceed.

Our first examination will be for a firm where industry statistics are available (Table 5.1). This table demonstrates a number of observable points and suggests several possible options:

- Relative to its total share of trade, Customer A is overtrading in the product-market in which the supplier operates and, relative to its overall share, the supplier is overtrading with this customer. Neither means that there is no room for scope, but insights are gained from having this knowledge.
- The other three customers are all undertrading in the supplier's product-market relative to their share of total trade. These percentages can be expressed as having a volume relationship. Further, volumes can be assigned a monetary value, which is more valuable when comparing possible candidates.
- The firm is undertrading with customers B, C and D.
- By a factor of 10, the greatest leverage lies in developing the customer's share of the supplier's product-market.

Three possible strategies suggest themselves:

- To work to help the customer expand its share of the firm's product categories while the firm simply tries to hold its percentage share of the customer's market. The result will be significantly higher revenues and contribution.
- As above, but simultaneously to try to build the percentage share of the customer's market. The result will be even bigger than above in both revenue and contribution, but the goal will be harder to attain.
- To try to increase the share of the customer's market irrespective of whether the customer's share of the total market goes up or down. The successful application of this strategy would mean increased revenues and contribution, but its impact would be diminished in relative terms by a factor of 10.

Table 5.1 Customer profiling – market share

	Customer A	Customer B	Customer C	Customer D
Customer's share of total market	10.3%	7.8%	5.5%	5.0%
Customer's share of product-market	11.3%	6.7%	3.0%	2.8%
Amount of over- or undertrading	(1.0%)	1.1%	2.5%	2.2%
Translated into units of volume	**(27 000)**	**27 500**	**62 000**	**58 000**
Firm's share of total market 7.7%				
Firm's share of customer's market	9.3%	5.9%	3.4%	6.8%
Amount of over- or undertrading	(1.6%)	1.8%	4.3%	0.9%
Translated into units of volume	**(2 400)**	**2 800**	**6 300**	**1 900**
Total theoretical potential in units of volume	**0**	**30 300**	**68 300**	**59 900**
Potential in value (£)	**0**	**4.55m**	**10.25m**	**8.99m**

Key:

'Customer's share of product-market' refers to the product-market in which the supplier operates.

'Amount of over- or undertrading' is the difference between total market share and product-market share. Overtrading is expressed in parentheses. All units of volume are theoretical.

'Potential in value' is obtained by multiplying selling price by volume, in this example at an average of £150 per unit.

The contribution factor cannot be judged since no information is given in the table. The specific strategy decision can come later. For now, we have half the answer to our earlier enquiry. Assuming a 10 per cent success rate, only Customer C passes the test. If we apply the assumption that a partnership would gain 15 per cent, Customers B and D also pass. Customer B comes in at around the 25 per cent mark.

Working from the belief that 25 per cent is attainable, we can proceed with three customers who have passed through the first filter. The ranking of these three candidates is also known:

1 Customer C
2 Customer D
3 Customer B

Customer A is not necessarily excluded at this stage, but the evidence suggests that the forces pushing against a sales development strategy on the part of either customer or supplier, or both, would be greater than the forces pushing forward. And a strong competitive response will drive market share increase costs up even faster than would otherwise be the case.

The second part of the equation must now be added. This means trying to answer two questions: first, how much extra revenue or contribution will arise as a result of new channels being opened, new product uses defined or as a direct result of a partnership initiative designed to expand the market? Secondly, how much of this increase could the firm reasonably hope to gain? The answers to these questions must be found both by extrapolating existing trends and looking into a crystal ball.

Erring on the side of caution, we can proceed by judging that various actions will add 2.5 per cent to the volume of the market if measured in 12 months' time. Will this 2.5 per cent affect the three customers equally? The answer to this is: only if no partnership effect is counted. If the 2.5 per cent increase is the result of a planned partnership, then it will arise wholly with one customer. The volumes and values are now added to the sum produced from Table 5.1 and a final first-hurdle result is shown.

The financial filter technique has, in fact, also taken account of one of the other 11 factors, that of share. In the calculations and evaluations needed to get three candidates through the first filter, the issue of market share was addressed at the same time. The filter was applied to an example where industry statistics were available, but there will be many instances where such data are limited or not available at all. In these cases, the same general guidelines should be followed as above, but a heavier reliance on management knowledge and judgement will be forced on the firm.

The second filter

The second screen to be applied to the three possible candidates is stability. We must attempt to assess this variable in two ways: financial stability and management decision stability. As before, the first measurement is quantifiable, the second is a management judgement. The first question to which an answer must be sought is: if resources are invested in developing a partnership with this customer, does the customer have sufficient financial stamina to see the initiative through to a mutually satisfactory conclusion?

Getting to an answer is normally fairly straightforward, particularly in publicly quoted firms. A few minutes spent studying the accounts, coupled with a pocket calculator to perform some simple ratio analysis, should provide all the data necessary to form an evaluation. There are some guidelines for using ratios that are important to understand if their application is not to be misused.

First, ratios should be seen as providing clues rather than specific answers. They point to issues requiring further examination. There are normally two occasions when the use of ratios is considered proper: to measure a firm's performance over time; and to build up a picture of the firm, again over a period of time. It is unsafe to use ratios to compare two firms, even if they seem to be similar, because even apparently similar firms will have enough differences to make the result unsound. There are hundreds of ratios, but we are chiefly concerned with those that can help determine the financial stability of a potential partner. For this reason, we will focus on ratios of stability.

Ratios of stability

The first test of a firm's stability is the current ratio. This examines the relationship between the firm's current assets and its current liabilities, and may be expressed as:

$$\text{Current ratio} = \frac{\text{Current assets}}{\text{Current liabilities}}$$

It used to be generally accepted that the current ratio should be 2 or better, meaning that if the total value of the firm's current assets is twice that of its current liabilities, it will be able to pay these liabilities as they fall due. This is a sign of financial stability over the next 12 months at least. It is clearly important, not only in terms of stability, but also as a measure of the confidence the firm's short-term creditors have in it. In recent years, the margin of safety has been reduced and a ratio of 1.5:1 is now thought of as being stable.

Calculating the ratio once will reveal little of significance; it must be calculated over a period of time. Fortunately, many annual reports now show three or more years. If the firm's current ratio is moving upwards over time, it is a healthy sign.

The current ratio has a deficiency that must be recognized. The ratio uses the three components of debtors, stock and cash, but two firms with the same ratio can have very different cashflow profiles. A firm might have high stocks that it has valued in its books at cost rather than realizable value. In a fire sale, the realizable value of the stocks may be only a fraction of their book value.

To overcome this problem, a second ratio, the acid test ratio, is used. This is expressed as:

$$\text{Acid test ratio} = \frac{\text{Current assets} - \text{Stock}}{\text{Current liabilities}}$$

This ratio tends to have a value range between 0.75 and 1.0, although it is quite common for firms to fall outside this range and yet still be stable.

The last stability ratio we will use is the working capital ratio. This relates working capital (current assets minus current liabilities) to sales, and is shown as:

$$\text{Working capital ratio} = \frac{\text{Working capital}}{\text{Sales} \times 100\%}$$

The range of possible values is wide, but a figure of between 20 and 33 per cent is common in manufacturing industry in the UK. The value of the working capital ratio will tend to fluctuate over time, but it will tell the same story as the acid test ratio.

These three ratios are used to determine a firm's stability, or liquidity. If they are worsening over time, or show a marked adverse difference between two accounting periods, a more thorough examination of the accounts should be undertaken to try to ascertain the reasons. It is important to see the ratios as indicators, where their relative value is greater than their absolute value.

In cases where the customer or supplier has no publicly available accounts to scrutinize, the use of ratios is clearly impossible and so a view must be formed as to the firm's stability from what is known of it as an insider. Firms suffering liquidity problems normally exhibit common characteristics, such as extending their supplier payment times or cancelling internal projects.

Management decision-making stability

By its nature, management decisions are subject to shifts of fortune caus-ing changes of direction from time to time. However, there is a marked and very significant difference between 'from time to time' and all the time. It is usually only by direct observation that an assessment of man-agement stability in this area can be reached. It is unwise to rely solely on third-party anecdotes, as these are almost certainly flavoured by per-sonal prejudice and opinion. Direct observation, either as a customer viewing a supplier at close range or the other way around, is not nor-mally too difficult.

The reason for this assessment being important is simple. A partner-ship candidate may be financially stable but managerially unstable. Unstable management has a tendency to make quixotic decisions, often based on the needs of the moment. If the needs of the moment change, so does the policy, and it is very difficult to develop a balanced partner-ship with a mercurial partner. What seemed to the customer an excellent partnership plan a few days ago now seems less so; if this triggers a knee-jerk response that adversely affects the partnership strategy in some way, it can have a rippling effect that lasts longer than the cir-cumstances that spurred the change.

History is often the best guide to the future, but the history in this case must be in relation to the managers who are in charge now. If the managers running the customer's or supplier's business have changed, it may have caused a change of policy at the same time which has nothing to do with instability of decision making. When management is broadly constant in make-up, however, history is a fair comparison with the present. Direct observation of customers and suppliers, preferably by more than one person, should be focused on the degree of constancy in strategic direction and decision making.

A candidate must pass both tests of stability to become eligible for further consideration. It is pointless to create a partnership with a company which is financially sound, but whose management is erratic. This is bound to lead to conflict sooner or later. If a firm passes on both counts, it is a worthy candidate for screening through the third filter.

The third filter

The third filter is almost entirely subjective. It is whether the prospec-tive partner is open-minded or, rather, whether its management is sufficiently open-minded to welcome new ideas and practices from out-siders. Some firms exhibit characteristics of open-mindedness, while others do not.

Open-mindedness means first of all a willingness to listen to opposing or different views, ideas and opinions. Secondly, it requires that there exist mechanisms to evaluate new ideas and practices, as well as the ability to incorporate the best ones. Open or closed minds can best be judged by direct observation of the way a firm behaves, but tangible evidence should be sought in every case.

The following list, though not exhaustive, will serve to illustrate what we are looking for:

- A stream of new products. This suggests a willingness to take risks in pursuit of greater rewards.
- The early introduction of new technology or management practices. Closed minds are more cautious, preferring to wait and see if something works before implementing it.
- Expansion into new product or service categories or new markets. This can usually be taken as a sign of forward thinking.
- The appointment of external managers as directors. External appointees are generally less risk averse than home-grown talent, as well as being more conscious of different and successful ways of working.
- Manifest changes in organizational structure, related to the adoption of a new strategy. Without this qualifier, there can be too many obfuscations in structural changes, because they may be made for many reasons other than a change in strategy; for example new senior managers wanting to make their mark, or top management trying to hide its failure in a reorganization.
- Evidence of acceptance and adoption of new methods, systems or procedures that arose from beyond the firm's structural boundaries, for example from consultants or simply from copying something observable or reported in another firm.

Open-mindedness is a vital ingredient in any partnership, mainly because the nature of the initiative should spawn many new ideas and, if any of these are to see the light of day, they must first be given thoughtful consideration. A partner whose ideas and suggestions are rejected without due care will soon become an unwilling participant.

Equally importantly, many people feel that change implies a degree of criticism of the present. And a manager who is an author of the way things are done at present may well develop feelings of defensiveness when presented with change. These will manifest themselves in an apparent unwillingness to adopt and internalize new ideas, thus closing the loop.

The two matters are rather different, although the result may seem the same. In the earlier category we have managers who refuse to hear new ideas because they believe that the current practice is the best practice, even though they have no proper yardstick. In the second group there are managers who are willing to consider new methods, but are afraid to try them. The distinction is an important one.

Given a choice between these two evils, it is relatively easier to work with people in a partnership when they are in the second group. Of course, the best option lies in having open-minded people.

The fourth filter

The fourth filter is a question of culture or, rather, of cultural fit between the two firms. Most studies of mergers and acquisitions stress the importance of culture, even though few people seem able to define it. It has been described as the 'management mindset' or 'management orientation', but both are too shallow to enable us to grasp the concept adequately. A simplistic, but perhaps sufficiently encompassing, idea of culture is to say that it is 'the stories and myths of the way things get done round here'. A new employee is subjected to an early taste of corporate culture, normally on the first day on the job, when a manager or supervisor begins explaining the firm's rituals and tells some of its stories.

Culture is just as real as the tables in the firm's coffee lounge. It exists everywhere in the firm at once and pervades every nook and cranny.

Corporate culture can alienate individuals and whole firms. At an individual level, alienated employees may leave, or stay and stick out like a sore thumb, while at the business-to-business level, firms can trade with one another but the relationship never becomes close. Equally, positive culture can bond individuals to the larger organization and firms to one another.

Writing about her experiences in one US firm in her book *The Change Masters*, Rosabeth Moss Kanter says:

> To manage such change as a normal way of life requires that people find their stability and security not in specific organizational arrangements but in the culture and direction of the organization. It requires that they feel integrated with the whole rather than identified with the particular territory of the moment, since that is changeable.

Our enquiry centres on the role played by corporate culture in the partnership context; here, the issue is how well or badly the two cultures fit together. We began by stating that a subjective assessment is necessary, because the scale and depth of work required for a more quantitative assessment would render the screening process unworkable. Having said this, there are instruments available which are relatively simple and inexpensive to use and which will illuminate this subject greatly.

There is another way to look at this question which makes it, per-haps, easier to answer in most cases. Is this a group of people with whom we want to develop a long-term and close relationship? Is there good or bad chemistry between us? Most people have instinctive or intuitive feelings about this, and they are often right. In the sense of personal relationships that are intended to be long lasting and close, most people choose others with whom they feel good chemistry. Defining it would be another matter, but that is not really what counts. What does count is the extent to which two individuals share these feel-ings and values. Business takes place between firms, but simultaneously at an individual level; it could not be otherwise. Therefore, it is the degree of shared feelings of good chemistry that determines the close-ness of the relationship.

Other considerations

From the original list of twelve factors we have applied six: financial, share, stability, open-mindedness, culture and chemistry. These factors form four filters and a firm passing successfully through these filters will be a suitable partnership candidate. However, there remain six other considerations that can be applied to the short list we have defined, and these are addressed below in the order first presented.

Education

This can be an inhibiting factor where either the general level of educa-tion or the specific level of management education is lacking on the part of either party to the agreement. In some cases the gap can be bridged, or relegated to a subordinate level of importance. In other cases it will assume a crucial, make-or-break role. An educational gap can also be perceived as a partnership opportunity. This can apply where one party has knowledge, skills, experience or competence that the other lacks. Provided it is presented in the right way, it can become a valid partner-ship entry point.

Technology

The same is true of technology. One firm may have obsolete technology, either in its fixed assets or its methods and procedures, which the other firm can help fill. A little caution may be advised here on occasion, since parasites exist in the corporate as well as the natural world.

Respect

This is a very important factor in any successful partnership. If the partners like one another as well, even better, but respect is a solid platform for trust and no partnership will last long without that.

Problems

Problems are universal; every firm has them. They can be a partnership gateway but, once more, some caution should be exercised. Particular care should be taken to avoid getting into a partnership based entirely on the resolution of a specific problem. The obvious risk is that once it has been resolved, the basis for the partnership no longer exists. Also, some problems are beyond the ability of one firm to solve. If the transport infrastructure in a particular geographic market is so rough as to make shipping costs prohibitive, even very powerful firms may baulk at tackling such a complex matter without government support.

Alliances

These can be the basis for a partnership in two ways. First, the organization seeking a partnership may be working as a partner with Firm A when Firm A decides to form an alliance with Firm B. This opens up another partnership opportunity. However, the same filters should be applied to Firm B irrespective of its links with Firm A. Secondly, the firm may see an opportunity to create a three-part alliance comprising itself, a supplier and a customer.

Management

The calibre of management in both partners will be one of the factors determining the speed at which ideas are adopted and progress made. This can be both an obstacle and an opportunity. It is an obstacle if the calibre of management in vital areas is so poor that progress is virtually impossible; an opportunity if there are calibre gaps on either side that the other can help close.

Using the four filters described above in conjunction with the other considerations will enable a short list to be drawn up from a long list of suppliers or customers. The most probable outcome is that the handful of candidates will be rank ordered by the filtering process, making the selection decision fairly simple. In a minority of cases, no rank order will suggest itself, leaving the final decision to be made by the application of management judgement. However, even in the relatively small number of cases where this happens, the judgement made will be considerably better informed.

Internal consultancy

Reference to the strategic partnership model shows that several steps are undertaken by the 'internal consultancy'. This is a group within the firm dedicated to the creation and application of a partnership with a specific supplier or customer. The group rarely exists on a full-time basis, but rather each member continues in his or her normal functional role, devoting some time to the internal consultancy group work. The formation of the group will vary from case to case, but we will use a customer-focused group as an example. This typically comprises the following people:

- *Account manager*. This sales or marketing person normally takes the leading role, because the job holder will ultimately spearhead the approach to the customer as well as leading the work that follows an agreement to proceed.
- *Finance specialist*. Since it is common for there to need to be some financial analysis and interpretation, someone with expert financial knowledge will be a great asset. The requirement for this expertise tends to grow as the partnership develops.
- *Systems specialist*. Given that much modern inter-company communication is by electronic means, and that partnerships are often a means of formalizing this, an expert systems person will be a vital ingredient. Different systems usually need to be made compatible and this is a job for an expert. The work tends to diminish to a maintenance role once the necessary programmes have been put in place.
- *Administrative support*. A great deal of information will be generated during the build-up to a partnership and it needs to be organized in order to release group members to concentrate on their specific tasks. The person providing the support also becomes an anchor to which other members can direct enquiries and information, thus ensuring a single data centre, rather than each member holding several pieces of the jigsaw puzzle.
- *Technical support*. Depending on the nature of the industry in which the firm operates, it will often be necessary to employ one or more technical experts in the internal consultancy. Their roles can only be determined by the nature of the industry and the intended scope of the partnership.
- *Champion*. Although not strictly a member of the internal consultancy group, each initiative must have a senior manager as its cham-

pion. The champion, or sponsoring executive, stays detached from the day-to-day work of the group, but offers advice and guidance when needed, as well as being the conduit to the board of directors for approvals and other decisions.

The internal consultancy group should be formed almost as soon as a partnership initiative is conceived. It will remain together, though not always with exactly the same composition, until the second customer commitment is gained. From this moment on, the group reforms itself into the nucleus of an SPI team and begins the partnership programme proper. This subject will be addressed in more detail in Chapters 9 and 10. Measures that can be taken later to build and strengthen the internal consultancy will be covered in Chapter 11.

Nothing much happens until someone makes a decision, and in this case the customer or supplier selection decision enables progression to the next stage of the partnership development process. We are now in a grey zone between completing the internal phase of the work and talking to the customer. What happens next will depend on whether a strategic partnership initiative has yet been identified, or whether this can only be unearthed by working with the potential partner.

Strategic partnership initiatives will be explored in the next chapter (Figure 5.1), but we can note at this point that an attractive SPI with one customer or supplier can make the final selection very straightforward. We will deal with this point in depth in Chapter 6.

Figure 5.1 The strategic partnership model excerpt

Strategic partnership initiatives

A strategic partnership initiative is the foundation on which a partnership can be started. It could be a commercial issue already facing both parties, although the degree to which it is recognized may differ. This is often due to differing impacts on supplier and customer. An SPI can also be an issue that has not yet surfaced, but that is likely to do so in the near future. A critical feature of SPIs is that they always have a profit impact.

The SPI is the vehicle through which partnership strategy is enacted. It is also the reason for the two firms to choose to work together in a special way. An SPI can also be an unresolved problem specific to one firm or to an entire industry, or it can be an opportunity that is there to be exploited. Either way, taken apart and reassembled, it becomes the partnership rationale.

An example on a large scale is European Monetary Union, which began in January 1999. Eleven countries formed the initial group, but the UK was not among them. Experts are unable to agree on much when EMU is discussed, but one consensus that has emerged is that the UK will be affected in any case. The scale of this impact, and whether it is uniform across UK industry, is open to debate, but many UK firms are taking it seriously enough to spend significant sums of money preparing for a second-wave entry. To illustrate the concept, here are two SPI possibilities arising directly out of European monetary policy aims:

■ A UK manufacturer of stainless steel sells 60 per cent of its output to EU countries. Before EMU, its costs arise in sterling and US dollars, because it has overseas raw material suppliers, but its prices are quoted in several different European currencies. These are later converted and consolidated into sterling, and the firm hedges its currency exposure risk by buying the appropriate instruments through its banking facilities. After 1 January 1999, the firm quotes for its European business in euros instead of several other currencies. Internally, managers believe that there is still an exposure to currency fluctuations, so its cost savings cannot yet be fully realized. However, there are some savings at the fringe and these are welcome. One of the steel producer's more powerful European customers tells it that it has become uncompetitive and that it must find ways to reduce its prices if it is to keep the customer. There are several ways the steel maker can tackle this challenge, but they fall into the two groups of confrontation or co-operation. It chooses the latter, and proposes a partnership to identify how the customer's input costs can be better managed.

■ A wholesale fish merchant in Belgium currently buys seafood from Spain, France, UK, Thailand, Canada and Malaysia as well as obtaining supplies locally. After 1 January 1999, its Far Eastern suppliers approach the firm and tell it that due to currency depreciation against the euro, they will be able to reduce their prices in return for a long-term contract for a greater share of the business. The merchant is interested in lower prices, but is aware of other risks too and wishes to maintain roughly the same balance of trade between European and non-European suppliers. The merchant has two broad choices: it can use the offer of lower prices to try to lever better terms from its European suppliers, or it can propose an initiative with some of its suppliers to form a group with the aim of ensuring supplies at stable prices in the future.

Five of the variables we looked at toward the end of Chapter 5 under the heading of 'Other considerations' can be the basis for an SPI at a more micro level.

An SPI must have four special characteristics:

1 It must be an issue of real interest and/or concern to the potential partner.
2 It must be a problem or a challenge that the potential partner has, to date, been unable to solve or respond to satisfactorily. However, short-term problem solving must be avoided, since it offers an opportunity to close the alliance down as soon as the problem has been solved.
3 It must offer a significant payoff to both parties. It is not always necessary or possible to quantify this in advance in precise terms.
4 The issue must be open ended. If there is a solution, it is not presently known to either prospective partner.

These characteristics form a list of criteria for evaluating whether an SPI is 'good' or 'bad'. It is good if it passes muster on all four counts; it is bad if it fails on any one. Only ideas that succeed in all four areas should receive further management attention, the aim of which will be to develop a detailed proposal.

It was observed at the end of Chapter 5 that we were in a grey zone in terms of whether the internal part of the partnership process had ended. This is because the basis for an SPI may not be known at the end of profiling and selecting a customer.

Identifying an SPI

There are three possible places from which an SPI can originate: from within the firm, from a customer or supplier, or from a third-party, external source. If the SPI originates internally, then its shape will probably be known at the end of the second step, profiling and selecting a partner. This can also be true of SPIs that originate from external third parties. Consultants, experts from trade bodies and other third-party agents may suggest something that signals the possibility of an SPI. Finally, an SPI immediately becomes known when the firm is approached by its supplier or customer with a proposal. This changes the focus somewhat, making it essential that the firm responds positively, either by accepting the proposal or entering into a negotiation as to how it could be developed in another way.

However, in many cases, an SPI will only emerge from detailed discussions with the supplier or customer who is the intended partner. In many instances, no obvious SPI suggests itself, or a half-seen shape emerges from discussions with the customer or supplier. This requires further discussion to explore what the issue is and how an SPI might help. With both of the last two possibilities, the external process has hardly begun and more discussions will be needed to identify a possible way ahead.

To summarize, four possibilities exist:

1 At the end of step 2, the firm knows the basis for an SPI. It now remains for it to work up the detail and form it into a proposal.
2 Alternatively, the firm is approached by one of its suppliers or customers. In either of these cases, the internal phase is complete. The two other possibilities below require more external discussion.
3 From earlier, non-specific discussions, the firm is half aware of a possible SPI. This will require more external discussion to identify and scope the opportunity prior to a full proposal being made.
4 An SPI can be suggested by an external third party, meaning that discussion with the hoped-for partner must follow to shape and scope the precise nature of the issue.

We looked earlier in this chapter at two big-picture examples of an SPI. Now we will further illustrate the concept with some examples at a business-to-business level:

■ In the provision of onscreen data in the financial services industry, a data supplier approaches a securities house customer with a proposal to work together to define the value of having 'intelligent' decision making with a human override built into dealing screen systems. If it merits it, the initiative would develop into a partnership whose object would be to show how the technical difficulties could be overcome.
■ A publisher discusses an initiative to speed up the supply of new material by setting up dictation lines on which existing and new authors can 'speak text' to a central computer. The initiative would

encompass the publisher, its authors, software writers and a third-party distributor such as British Telecom. Phase one of the initiative would be a feasibility study.

- A manufacturer of heavy earthmoving equipment, with customers all over the world, backed up by extensive distribution and after-sales service networks, develops an initiative with selected key distributors simultaneously to speed up the delivery of spare parts and to reduce inventory costs.
- Psychologists working in the field of stress at work formulate a proposal to work with selected groups of managers and staff in the ambulance and fire services to ascertain the causes and cost of stress and suggest methods to reduce it. Partners in such a study would be the employers and employees of the two services, labour unions and outside experts.
- A supplier of fertilizers and other soil-treatment chemicals suggests a partnership with a group of farmers, through a local branch of the National Farmers' Union. The initiative will look at ways in which the fertilizers and their application on the farm can be made 'greener'.
- A grocery products supplier starts an initiative with a retail chain to identify the reasons for the difference between what consumers say they plan to buy when they visit the retailer's stores and what they actually do purchase when they get there.
- Consultants propose a project to a client to make a detailed study of all its subsidiary operating units. The purpose of the study is to find ways to effect savings of 10 per cent in total costs.
- A major retail chain proposes that one of its key suppliers assumes responsibility for managing an entire section of electrical power tools, of which it is a manufacturer. The supplier will be given a free hand, with the retailer simply insisting on a steady margin improvement.
- In the glassmaking industry, a supplier proposes an alliance to examine new resins and bonding materials to explore how they will change the nature and application of the customer's product range.
- Two cross-Channel ferry operators agree to start an initiative to examine how routes could be merged to reduce operating costs and compete more favourably with the Channel Tunnel and with airlines.

Each of these examples would need to be fleshed out before a decision as to their feasibility could be made, but they serve here to illustrate the range of potential avenues that exist for partnership strategies.

Two other examples were offered in Chapter 2, although no mention of an SPI was made at that time because the discussion was in a different context. These were expertise in promotional activity for an FMCG supplier and a retail customer, and space logistics for an automotive parts supplier dealing with motor manufacturers.

Bases for identifying SPI opportunities

There are two generic ways in which an SPI may be identified, which may be described as problems and challenges, either of which may be peculiar to one firm or applicable to an entire industry. Remember, though, that people will see problems and challenges quite differently, depending on which side of the desk they sit and their level of seniority.

One way of locating possible grounds for an SPI is through existing problems or those likely to arise in the near future. There are two ways in which this can happen.

First, an SPI may be a customer or supplier problem which has not yet been recognized or the impact of which has not fully been appreciated. It is, however, recognized by the other party, which proposes working together to try to resolve it. Secondly, a problem in one firm may be recognized by both but, as yet, neither has suggested a partnership initiative to try to find a workable solution. These kind of problems typically exist between one firm and another and are generally specific to one of the firms concerned. Therefore, a supplier may have a shipping problem that affects all its customers, though not necessarily to the same degree.

Equally, a firm can have a challenge to which it has no present strategy. For example, the market in which it operates may be growing by 10 per cent in volume terms per annum, but its sales are rising at half that rate. In another case, current practice may be adequate, yet resolution of a particular technical, production or logistics challenge would open opportunities for the firm to gain leadership over its rivals.

A second means of finding SPI opportunities relates to industry-wide considerations. These are situations where the industry as a whole faces an issue that needs to be resolved. Its impact on firms in the industry varies from firm to firm, but all face it in one way or another. An example would be a recession specific to one industry rather than to the entire economy. There are many instances of this, but the UK coalmining sector or the mainly northern-based cotton-dyeing industry, declining in the face of cheap imports from Asia, are two examples. The plight of Britain's beef farmers during the past few years is another obvious case in point. These three matters are quite obviously major challenges for everyone concerned in these product-markets. Whether they can be resolved satisfactorily without state intervention is questionable and caution would be urged before embarking on such a venture. There is no doubting the scale of eventual payoff resulting from a successful partnership, but the risk of failure must not be overlooked.

Challenges do not always have to be difficulties, however. The challenge of increasing total consumption of drinking water would be positive to water producers, packaging materials suppliers, retailers and other distributors. In many industries, so too would be the challenge of finding ways to manufacture on the move as a way of reducing lead times and inventory costs. A glance at the examples given above as well as those in Chapter 2 will reveal the category into which they should be placed.

Shaping an SPI

Identifying a possible SPI is the beginning of this part of the work. Now it must be shaped so that it meets the specific needs of the chosen customer or supplier. These needs will fall into one or both of the following classes: they will be either personal or corporate. The fulfilment of personal needs appeals to individuals within the firm, while corporate needs are fulfilled by meeting the firm's strategic goals. If the target firm is a small to medium-sized entrepreneurial business, personal needs may sometimes take precedence. This is because in firms of this type, personal needs are often uppermost in the owners' thoughts, or are indistinguishable from the needs of the firm. In the majority of cases, however, corporate needs will be most important.

The factors discussed in Chapter 5 in relation to profiling and selecting a partner will provide many clues to how to shape the SPI to increase its appeal to the potential partner. However, some special variables must now be overlaid to complete the picture, some of which are clearly situations to be avoided. The order in which these variables will be considered will, to some extent, depend on each unique set of circumstances; however, the ranking used below is typical of the approach required.

Timing

Is the prospect ready to begin working in a partnership? There may be other initiatives under way at present which use up a large portion of resources and management attention. However well shaped the SPI, it will not be as successful if it has to compete for attention with too many other strategies. A decision to defer approaching the target because of the answer to this question does not invalidate the work carried out in Chapter 5, it merely postpones it.

Whether the firm now moves its second choice to the top of its list will depend on how far back the timing issue with the first choice has to be pushed. Secondly, the firm may decide to approach its prospective partner now, but propose that any initiative agreed is not commenced until both partners are ready. This strategy contains some dangers, however, foremost among which is the shifting sand of business priorities that forever shuffles the initiative to the back of the pack.

Takeovers

It is generally best to avoid letting a partnership initiative become entangled in a merger or acquisition. Once again, so much management attention will be focused elsewhere that the SPI will not receive the support necessary to sustain it. Of course, there are instances where it is unavoidable; for example an SPI is started, only for a merger to be announced later. In these cases there are only two options: continue, but perhaps at a slower rate; or park the initiative until the dust settles. As we have seen, however, a merger or acquisition, in either direction, can be the catalyst for a new partnership. Once more, timing is crucial.

Downsizing

Implementing action on this front again ties up a great deal of management time and energy. It is also usually coupled with there being fewer managers around to carry through partnership-building activities. Finally, there is often a surfeit of negative energy in downsizing situations, and it is best to avoid the risk of this being targeted against the partnership as a means of 'getting back' at the employer making the staff reductions.

Adoption

This relates to the level of acceptance of the partnership concept and the speed with which it will be adopted by various functions and hierarchical levels of the second party to the agreement. Different parts of a firm can simultaneously pursue different objectives, and will occasionally employ blocking tactics against projects judged to be contrary to functional interests. As we shall see later, measures will be taken to reduce this risk, though it can never be eliminated entirely. Speed of adoption will also be influenced by the degree of experience among managers and staff in using different working practices and procedures, and by the method and quality of the briefing that takes place.

Knowhow

It is vital that all members of the internal consultancy team responsible for developing the internal steps of the project to date, as well as planned future additions to the team once the initiative starts, are conversant with the theory and practice of developing strategic partnerships. In addition, the supervising managers must be even more familiar with its practice, since it is they who will be responsible for guiding the team through the various stages of partnership implementation.

Trust

It is common when commencing a strategic partnership for there to be limited or varying degrees of trust. This is especially true when the proposal emanates from a supplier. Members of customer management and staff will, in some cases, believe that it is just another 'angle' to get closer to an important customer. In certain cases, based on past experience, they will be right. This is very unfortunate, since it makes the task harder for those who follow, even those bent on a more authentic methodology. However, programmes that start from an ethical base will normally overcome these early difficulties. It must be remembered, nevertheless, that trust cannot be taken for granted in any partnership. It has to be earned and built up in small incremental steps.

As with any business venture, there are risks to a partnership strategy, but if sufficient thought is given to these aspects of partnership planning, the difficulties and perceived risk will be at least minimized.

The customer contact plan

Recalling that in the majority of cases we are still in the internal planning phase, it is time to bend our thinking to the various contacts, at different hierarchical levels, that must be made in order to gain customer or supplier approval to the initiative. Once more, reference to the strategic partnership model shows that the next step triggers off a kill point. However, before reaching that point, we must first consider the customer contact plan. And in doing so, we arrive at a key principle of the whole partnership approach.

Partnerships are a matter of strategy, not operational tactics which are decided and implemented by middle management. Strategy, on the other hand, is determined by top management and acted on by managers down the line. Therefore a partnership strategy, like any other strategy that a firm employs, must be approved and supported by top management if it is to succeed. Further, this approval and support should be sought at the very outset of the initiative. There are several good reasons for this:

- Acceptance of the partnership proposal will have to come from top management. They might as well see it first. This has the added benefit of smoothing the path at other organizational levels.
- Top management approval removes at a stroke the uncertainty felt by other managers who, if they see the proposal first, will be unsure whether it will ultimately gain approval or not.
- The most likely place for partnership proposals to be blocked is at middle management level. The news that a partnership will be entered into can remove, reduce or increase the negative energy which can sometimes be directed against change, in whatever form it comes. In the latter case, the firm must address itself to removing negative energy blockages before they poison the atmosphere.
- Much valuable time can be wasted talking to people who cannot make partnership decisions. Many people may like the idea, but if they lack board approval they can do nothing.
- Part of the agenda of strategic partnerships is to create stronger bonds between the two respective top management tiers. The process should begin as quickly as possible.

Although the reasons for starting at the top are overwhelming, there are two apparent risks attached. The first is that the proposal is turned down, thus closing off any further hope, at least for the moment, of developing a partnership with this customer or supplier. In reality, it is better to know this at the beginning rather than wasting time and money pursuing a lost cause. The other risk is of alienating the middle-ranking managers whose support will be needed once the actual work commences. Alienation, it is sometimes argued, can be caused by 'going behind the buyer's back'. This is a spurious argument, since top managers in different firms talk to each other all the time, about a broad range of business topics affecting their firms or their industry. This is just one other occasion. In any case, buyers cannot normally make decisions affecting strategy. If someone is piqued by an approach to senior managers, it becomes another issue to be managed as part of developing and building a strategic partnership.

Creating a customer contact plan requires a timetable and a reporting mechanism. The timetable should specify who will contact whom, by when and in what sequence. The reporting mechanism alerts everyone involved that a contact has been made, and that the process is either stalled or the next contacts in the planned sequence may now take place. Both these requirements can be satisfied in one simple document (Table 6.1).

Table 6.1 Customer contact plan

Name and title	Contact	No	By when	Result and next action
Terry Gough Managing director	Managing director	1	30 Oct	Meeting with Terry Gough on 21 Oct successful. Has agreed to partnership in principle, subject to study. Tate & Jones to be seen.
Paul Tate Production manager	Commercial director	2	14 Nov	
Alan Jones Operations manager	Commercial director	3	14 Nov	
Production and operations supervisors	Commercial director and internal consultancy	4 5?	22 Dec	

This example is an abbreviated version of what would actually be required. It is impossible to say how many names a real contact list would contain, but it must show everyone who falls into the two categories discussed below.

The example demonstrates that a list of contacts has been created, that the managing director of the proposing firm has contacted the managing director of the intended partner, and that approval has been gained to move the process along, that this will now be followed up by the commercial director contacting named personnel, and that perhaps two further meetings must take place in order to see everyone else whose support will be needed.

The document is created as soon as the prospective partner has been identified, but before any external contacts are made. The only exception to this rule is when the firm is approached by one of its suppliers or customers. Even here, we must be certain that the idea has board support within the firm initiating the proposal before committing resources.

It is still essential that the personnel who are likely to affect the outcome of the partnership are identified before commencing contacts.

Although a partnership should not be proposed without senior-level approval on both sides, its success depends on much more than this. As partnerships unfold, more and more people become involved at various hierarchical levels in both firms and so success rests on many shoulders. The customer contact plan therefore serves two purposes:

1 To identify various 'permission givers'. These are the people, starting at board level, who must give permission for the initiative to be taken a stage further. Department heads are other obvious permission givers.
2 To categorize decision makers and influencers. These will be grouped under the various parts of the partnership where decisions must be made or can be influenced. For instance, a department head in personnel may not make many decisions directly affecting the partnership, but can heavily influence its outcome by fact of hierarchical position. Conversely, a junior person working in a technical capacity may have a great deal of decision-making power in a limited technical sphere, but none elsewhere.

Once the customer contact plan has been created, we have definitely reached the end of the internal part of the partnership process and can now begin to focus our energy on the prospective partner. So far, we will have identified and selected that partner, whether customer or supplier, will quite possibly have an SPI in mind, and will have a sequenced list of people who must be seen and persuaded. It is now time to contact the customer or supplier.

This means turning the customer contact plan into action. The person to whom the initial contact task has been assigned must contact the designated person of authority and arrange a meeting. A telephone call is often the simplest and fastest way to get in touch, although in some cases a more formal approach is best and a letter must be sent first.

Either way, some notion of the purpose of the meeting and its structure will help. It is unlikely in any case that senior people will have the time or inclination to attend meetings when they have no idea what is to be the purpose of the discussion. So a brief explanation of the agenda is not only good practice, it helps the other person decide if others should attend. Avoid filling in too much detail: it gives the impression that the answers are already known. Generalized statements related to the specifics of how the two firms do business together, or how the supplier interfaces with its customers, will normally suffice. Make it clear that the proposed meeting format will be a presentation, which elevates the meeting a peg above the normal.

Refusal to agree to a meeting is obviously a kill point (Figure 6.1), but we must assume that the prospective partner feels sufficiently tempted by what is said on the telephone or in a letter to agree to meet. In fact, the meeting itself brings us to the second kill point, because it moves the two firms towards a decision that will either take the process forward or kill it off. The former will simultaneously be a joint statement of commitment.

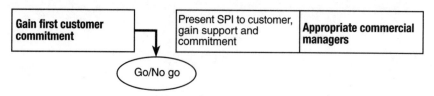

Figure 6.1 The strategic partnership model excerpt

Part III
Implementing and Sustaining an Alliance

Gaining partnership commitment

We begin this chapter with a reminder that a true strategic partnership cannot exist without demonstrable commitment on both sides, and the point has now been reached when that commitment must be given and obtained. Gaining the commitment of a prospective partner relies on that party fully understanding what is being asked and what a partnership commitment might involve. Getting someone to agree to a proposal in business usually means giving information, answering questions and painting a picture of a potentially brighter future. Since few people have time to waste, being concise is important too, and this is also a good discipline to learn since it helps concentrate thinking on key topics when planning and conducting the meeting.

The aim of setting up a meeting with a prospective partner is to agree to do something together and, as a minimum, to end the meeting with an agreement to proceed to the next stage. Failure to gain that agreement kills off the prospective partnership then and there, at least until such time as a commitment is forthcoming. This is a crucial principle of strategic partnerships and will bear repetition. Moving on to the next step in building a partnership must not be a one-sided affair. It must only take place with the commitment of both prospective partners. If the party receiving the proposal infers or states that the proposing firm may go ahead with the next step in the process alone, the scheme should be jettisoned on the spot. To go ahead on your own would be rather like inviting someone to join an exclusive club offering many benefits and then saying that the subscription fee will be waived. Such an offer would cheapen the invitation.

Two factors can make a partnership proposal easier to accept: first, the customer or supplier is not being asked to swallow the whole meal in one sitting; and secondly, the commitment asked for is relatively inexpensive. The proposal is not to sign up to a full partnership right away, but to bite off one piece to try. This piece is the technical and commercial study, a subject which will be dealt with in the next chapter. Full partnership commitment will only be sought after the study has been completed and provided that it shows that a partnership will be mutually beneficial. Furthermore, there are no free rides in a real partnership and the prospective partner might as well learn that maxim right now.

The usual way in which one firm persuades another to change strategy and embark on a partnership is through a formal, structured presentation, and this is also the case here. In this chapter, we will examine the guidelines, format and structure of a partnership presentation, and explore the differences between it and normal business presentations. We will begin by looking at the main components of a partnership presentation and will then review an example case.

Partnership presentations

Presentations are part of the lifeblood of organizational life. Most managers are used to making and receiving them but they need to be carefully planned to be effective. The planning of a partnership presentation should start with these six questions:

1 What is the purpose of this presentation?
2 Who will be involved?
3 What will be said and how?
4 Where will it be said?
5 What is expected next?
6 What course can be followed if the meeting fails?

What is the purpose of this presentation?

This is simple. The objective is to give and gain commitment to a strategic partnership, explaining the specific benefits along the way. Within the overall purpose, partnership presentations have three subobjectives:

■ To show that the firm understands a particular issue or problem.
■ To put across a strategy encompassing a possible solution, provided that the solution proposed is sufficiently flexible to allow plenty of scope.
■ To persuade the audience to 'buy in' to the proposed solution.

The first is often overplayed and, when this happens, it is usually at the cost of the second and third.

Who will be involved?

Since the approach will have been from one senior manager to another, part of the answer is clear. However, two further possibilities emerge at this point: one is that the senior person to whom the proposal is to be put will be alone, and the other is that one or more colleagues will be invited. The firm's response should be to accept either situation and to tailor numbers accordingly. In the first case, only one person, at most two, should attend from the firm's side. In the latter case, numbers may be higher, but only those with something to contribute should be there. The firm's representatives will be the 'appropriate commercial managers' as seen in the strategic partnership model.

Other factors to consider are:

■ Why are they here?
■ What do they want out of it?
■ How much do they already know?
■ Are they experts or novices in the subject matter?
■ How do they feel towards the firm?
■ What assumptions have they made about the firm?
■ What do they want/expect to be offered?
■ Who are the decision makers?
■ Who are the key influencers?

It is important to know the audience – or, at least, to know as much about their needs as possible. Often a great deal will be known in advance, with people talking to others they know, but on other occasions people will be meeting for the first time. This should not be an issue as long as some simple guidelines, outlined later in this chapter, are followed.

What will be said and how?

The structure of the partnership presentation will be covered in depth in this chapter, but for the moment we can concentrate on another aspect of the question. This is what the listeners expect to hear. They will know something of the topic in advance because it will have been stated in the telephone call or letter that set up the meeting. In addition, we can reasonably expect that they are busy people and that they are used to hearing business presentations. Most people are affected positively by well-thought-out and structured arguments, and negatively by poorly constructed ones. Therefore, the 'how' must meet the three criteria of professional, polished and persuasive.

Where will it be said?

In the majority of cases, the meeting will take place at the customer's or supplier's offices. If this is so, remember a few simple tips:

■ Find out in advance what equipment is going to be available. This will allow a presentation to be designed around the existing facilities more effectively. If you have technical gadgets you plan to use, check whether you need permission to bring them into the building.

- Find out when access to the room will be possible. It will be of benefit to get the feel of the place before beginning the meeting, as well as ascertaining the position of equipment in advance.
- Ask whether any special seating arrangements are preferred. It would be a pity to ruin a good argument by inadvertently sitting in the host managing director's favourite chair.

There will be other instances when the opportunity of selecting a venue arises. Choosing the venue or, rather, choosing the *right* venue is an important part of the presentation. The style, appearance and ambience of the surroundings will have an effect on your audience and, therefore, on how your argument is received. Here are some tips to remember when booking and preparing a venue:

- If it is possible to conduct the presentation at your own premises, do so. It means you have more control and there is less risk of things going wrong.
- Avoid a large physical gap between presenters and audience. Within reason, the closer people are to each other, the easier it will be for them to see and hear – which is what they have come for.
- If a venue is being used with which not everyone is familiar, like a hotel, make sure that the meeting room is well signposted from the reception area, and that hotel receptionists have been briefed on where to direct people.
- Brand the room. This is a vital discussion with important customers or suppliers, so make an effort to brand the room with some materials that stamp your unmistakable personality on it. This might include discreet wall signs, notepads carrying the firm's logo or name cards, as well as the customer's or supplier's logo prominently displayed.
- Make sure that there is access to the room some time before the presentation commences. This allows time to make sure everything is in order and get the 'feel' of the room.
- If electronic presentational aides are to be used, check everything carefully: plugs, cables, extension leads, video players (don't forget the tape), overhead projectors (spare bulb/whether it works), whether someone knows how to fix anything that breaks down.
- Decide which side of the room to present from; this could be important. If the room being used is on the ground floor and opposite the hotel swimming pool, people's attention could be distracted from time to time.
- Position any visual aids for use during the meeting where they can be reached without leaning over a table or tripping over cables. In small

rooms, a colleague can be briefed to help by switching a projector on and off, for instance.

What is expected next?

Don't let your listeners have to guess what's going to happen – tell them. A commitment is required to enable the project to move forward. In fact, two commitments will be asked for:

- The customer or supplier must agree to meet at some future date, after the technical and commercial study has been completed and its results analysed and assessed, to hear what actions might begin a formal partnership. It is essential that this second presentation is made to the same top management personnel as attend the first meeting. The commitment asked for will be their attendance; the date can be sorted out later.
- Secondly, the customer or supplier must commit some people to work on the technical and commercial study. Typically, these studies take place over several weeks, adding up to perhaps 10 days' work, plus some time to digest what has been learned and plan the second presentation. The prospective partner must supply someone as a liaison between the two firms during the study and, sometimes, during the analysis and assessment as well. These points will be developed fully in the next chapter.

It has already been stated that a true strategic partnership is one in which both partners have demonstrated their commitment. In one sense, the firm has already demonstrated its commitment by engaging in all the preparatory work required to get to this meeting, but, of course, that is all invisible to the other side. Now it is time for the two parties to commit to something visible and tangible. The customer or supplier will be asked for both of the commitments above, and the proposing firm must commit to carrying out the study needed to establish the boundaries of a future partnership. As we have seen, studies typically require 10 working days, plus analysis time. It is probable that several people from the firm will be involved in the study and, occasionally, outside experts as well.

This clearly has a significant cost. It is this cost, above and below the line, to which the firm must commit, irrespective of whether the partnership goes ahead afterwards or not. This should be made clear at the presentation, because it places in its proper context the relatively minor commitment that the customer or supplier is being asked to make. Equally, it begins to frame the picture regarding statements of mutuality and fairness that are vital for any partnership to succeed over the long haul.

What course can be followed if the meeting fails?

By 'fails', we means fails to achieve any commitment from the other side. There are two possibilities in this case: that the prospect needs more time to consider the position; or that they state their refusal to participate at the end of the meeting. If the former is applicable, try to agree a time by when a decision can be expected. In the second instance, there is a failure, no mistake. The course of action is simple: put this one down to experience, analyse what went wrong with the selection process and move on to the next target.

Planning the partnership presentation

The real difficulty occurs when you are planning the initial partnership presentation. Everything must be brought together for the first time. On second and subsequent occasions, much of the material will already have been prepared, but of course the customer or supplier specifics must be added each time. The following tips can be applied to the planning of an entire partnership presentation for the first time and to specific parts of it for more experienced users.

Begin with the idea-generation phase. This can be done by one person, but it often helps if others are involved. Mind mapping is a useful technique since it is fast and simple, although some people prefer to write copious notes and work from these. An excellent guide to the mind-mapping technique is to be found in *Use Your Head* by Tony Buzan.

Mind mapping starts by writing the objective in the centre of a piece of blank paper – A3 is best, but A4 will do – then working through all the ideas that seem connected to it. Do not stop to evaluate anything: it is more important to think through all the potential elements of the presentation first. Use line branches connected to the centre. Write key words on these branches, connecting others as it develops. Colour helps, since the eye–brain combination will sort by colour before anything else. Any rough drawings or symbols created as the map develops will help recall the need for visual aids at a later stage.

As well as generating ideas, study the material to find the core message and the structural elements that support it. In using this technique or one similar to it, the authors are seeking to do five things, either in one session or, more likely, over several:

1 Get everything that seems as if it could be relevant written down as quickly as possible.
2 Find the core message. This will ultimately be one or two sentences at the heart of the presentation, which contain the central idea of the

proposal. For example, 'Higher productivity results from motivated people' or 'Quality management saves money without having to make or sell another thing'. The core message should bring the objective to life. 'To persuade you to be our partner' might better be phrased as 'Strategic partnerships can be more rewarding in many ways'. The 'here's how' bit is contained in the structure.

3 Working from the notes created earlier, find the key elements that support the core message, and begin arranging these into 'statement sets' in a sequence that seems to make sense and that would be easy for others to follow.
4 Tighten the statement sets into a concise argument by going over the storyline several times alone and with colleagues.
5 Identify any visuals that will be needed during the presentation.

The presentation structure

The structure is the vehicle that carries the key message. Structure is needed because if a partnership presentation consisted of nothing more than a core message statement, more questions would be triggered off than could be answered. Structure also sets an overall context and enables an argument to be better understood. It should not simply be a logic flow or sequence flow. It is not even a convenient way to group a set of ideas. It is the entire argument that conveys your point of view as persuasively as possible. Here is an example:

Core message
We must change the way we operate if we are to stay ahead of our competitors, remain in healthy profitability and keep everyone fully employed. A partnership is one way of doing this.

Structure
■ Why our market share may be in danger.
■ What we need to do to maintain it.
■ What our competitors are doing.
■ Which strategies are worth consideration.
■ Why a partnership strategy would suit us.
■ We need to find a good partner.

In this example, the structure is divided into six separate but linked sections. Each segment supports the whole, and the whole is the sum of the core message. To find a structure from an original set of notes, begin by referring to the map and proceed by crossing out the key points as they are worked into the presentation structure. Don't worry if some points on the map have to be discarded as long as their omission does not weaken the structure. Next, group ideas into sections. These become the sections of the presentation. Thirdly, look to see if there are points which do not fit the structure, but which should be included. If this is the case, amend the structure.

Scripting

There should now be a working structure for the presentation. The next decision involves the best way to prepare the script. There are several options:

1 Memorize every word.
2 Write out the whole script in longhand or have it typed.
3 Use prompt cards.
4 Use a single-sheet map similar to the original mind map.
5 Talk from the visuals.

Memorizing every word is very difficult and is made harder when more than one person is presenting. It has the advantage of making people sound natural, but the real flaw is that of a serious risk of forgetting something. Writing or typing the presentation out makes it hard to read without being tremendously boring, and risks losing the attention of the people who must be persuaded. Using prompt cards (small cards on which key words are written) can help avoid the pitfalls mentioned above. The same applies to the last two options. The decision depends on several factors, key among which are the professionalism of the presenter and the receptiveness of the audience. Remember, however, that the latter will be influenced by the former. In the end, there is no substitute for knowing the material inside out, and that means rehearsing it thoroughly.

Presentation format

Partnership presentations, like interviews or meetings, should have a beginning, a middle and an end. Although they will vary in style and content, there are some simple ground rules to follow:

■ Include an introduction and welcome. Introduce the speakers and anyone else there. The level of the introduction will, of course, depend on how well people know one another. Welcome your audience and thank them for giving valuable time to attend. Explain the speaker's credentials and why they are giving this presentation. Explain whether you will take questions during the presentation or at the end. During is always better because it makes for better interaction.

■ Outline the subject matter. Tell people what it is you are going to tell them, explaining briefly what is in it for them. Outline the structure and content to be covered, saying roughly how much time will be needed. If an SPI is known in advance, refer to this now. Begin at the first part of the planned structure and work through to the end.

■ When the end is reached, summarize briefly what has been said and how it benefits them. Describe hoped-for future actions, on both sides.

Performance skills

Speakers must project themselves if their ideas and views are to be persuasive and convincing to others. They should appear confident, relaxed and natural. This is far from easy for most people, but being aware of a variety of performance factors will help:

■ *Keep to ordinary words.* Try to speak as you do in everyday language with colleagues and friends. Use language that the audience will understand. It is possible to get away with poor grammar or syntax in a spoken presentation, even slang can be used – but don't overdo it. Learn to speak clearly.

■ *Deliver naturally.* The chances are that by adulthood, your speech delivery and accent are relatively fixed. Don't try to change them too much.

■ *Use normal mannerisms.* Everyone has them, but they are not awkward in presentations unless they are so pronounced that they irritate or give offence. On the contrary, mannerisms reflect the natural person. Colleagues will point out any mannerisms that need to be eradicated. Make gestures positive but non-threatening. It is important that they are in keeping with what is being said, or there is a danger that they will simply be distracting for the audience.

■ *Keep up the pitch of your voice.* Dropping your voice at the end of sentences is a common mistake and suggests a lack of confidence. Emphasize key words and phrases by keeping your voice pitch high. This is especially valid when enunciating the benefits of a partnership.

■ *Pause after key points.* A short pause can be more effective than anything else in reinforcing the previous point. Pauses also allow both speaker and listeners to gather their thoughts and catch up.

■ *Vary delivery speed.* Avoid becoming locked into a standard delivery rate. Try to vary it according to what is being said. Slowing down adds weight to a point. Most people need to slow down their presentation speed by 10–20 per cent.

■ *Use repetition.* Repetition can be used in two valuable ways: a single word or phrase can be repeated for emphasis; and a significant point may be made more than once during the presentation. Repetition is a well-known memory aid.

■ *Keep good posture.* Stand square to the audience, otherwise it will be difficult to make regular eye contact with the people immediately to the left and right sides. The lower part of your body should be firm but relaxed and the upper part erect.

■ *Use your hands.* Hands can be embarrassingly awkward. Use one to hold a pointer and the other to gesticulate to support key points. Be careful with an international audience. Find out if any particular gestures have an offensive meaning. In any case, don't point with your fingers. Keep your hands out of your pockets, or at least remove any loose change first. Leave your bag somewhere safe, not swinging on your shoulder.

■ *Don't take root.* Natural movement benefits the presenter, so don't be afraid to move your feet and body. It helps reinforce a key point if a step forward is taken as the main words are spoken. This is made possible by stepping back a pace moments earlier. Find a comfortable standing position, shifting your weight from one foot to the other for a while before returning to your original position. Try to make your movements reflect your words.

■ *Use signposting.* This is one of the most important of all presentation skills. Signposting is what it suggests, giving others an indication of where they are being taken in the presentation. The first signpost normally comes during the introduction when the presenter explains the components to be covered. The number of times signposting should be used depends on the length and complexity of the presentation, but it generally cannot be overused. Visuals can also fulfil this purpose.

■ *Maintain eye contact.* This is a very important ingredient of the presentation. Try to achieve a 'lighthouse beam' effect. Don't look for a friendly face and fix on this person, or contact will be lost with the rest of the audience, missing any signals they might give out. Good eye contact is the most powerful sensory pathway to the brain. Look at everyone in the audience. It is much better to be looking at the audience than at the floor, ceiling or visuals.

■ *Group items in threes for emphasis and ease of explanation.* Partnership presentations are complex and typically have five to eight structural sections. This can make the concept hard to grasp for someone hearing it for the first time, so reinforcement by grouping key points in threes will help. It is widely accepted among professional speakers that clustering items in threes is the best number to give reinforcement to each point without confusing an audience with too many points.

■ *Summarize frequently*. This is the other side of the signposting coin. If signposting points the way ahead, summarizing describes where you have been. There should be a short summary at the end of each section, highlighting the key points of that section, and a final summary at the end that encompasses the highlights.

Attention span

The attention span of an audience will to an extent be affected by the quality of the presentation. However, it is generally believed that full attention will last for about 10 minutes, then drops off quite sharply, and returns to a high level of concentration for the last few minutes as people sense that the end is nigh. Even for the best presenter, attention is rarely kept at a high level for long. This has the obvious danger that a key point will be missed.

Gaining audience involvement is highly beneficial in keeping attention. It breaks the invisible barrier between speaker and audience and gets everyone on the same wavelength. A joke is one way to do this, but it is recommended only for highly experienced speakers. Jokes can go badly wrong and there is nothing less funny than a joke at which no one laughs. There are better and safer techniques:

■ One way to gain involvement is through questions. Questions to which the only answer is 'Yes' are perfect. Rhetorical questions are ideal, particularly where it is inappropriate to expect a member of the audience to reply. It is a good idea when addressing questions to an individual or to the group in general to frame the question in the context of a common or shared experience.
■ Ask the audience about the way they do things at the moment. This encourages direct involvement and generally means that others will pay attention to the reply. This is especially true when the boss is speaking.
■ Ask what alternatives they have considered. This has the same effect as the point above, but forces someone in the audience to reply.
■ Ask them about their order of priorities. Get them involved. This is a useful technique at specific points in the presentation when interest seems to be waning.
■ Use memorable words, names or phrases.
■ Summaries usually arouse attention, because people often assume that the summary will include all the key points they might have missed the first time around.

Summarizing and concluding

The end of the presentation is just as important, perhaps more so, than the beginning. What is said and done at the end may be all that people remember afterwards. One of the main distinctions between partnership presentations and what we might term 'normal' business presentations is that in the former decisions are usually made at a later date, when the presenter cannot be there to influence the outcome. It is therefore vitally important to work out what will be said and who will say it. It is also a good idea to memorize the ending. This will allow the presenter to maintain good eye contact, giving greater emphasis and impact.

Here are a few simple rules for ending presentations:

■ Briefly summarize all the key points.
■ If there is one visual which synthesizes the firm's view, use it.
■ Keep the ending simple and 'tell 'em what you told 'em'.
■ Restate the core message.
■ Tell them what should happen next.

In covering the last point, specify the action the firm would like to see and the timescale, if appropriate. Distribute any handouts together with a brief explanation of the information contained in them. Thank the audience for their patient attention. Invite them to ask other questions.

Rehearsing

Once it has been planned and structured, the partnership presentation should be rehearsed often enough to enable speakers to deliver it with complete confidence. Sometimes it is valuable to rehearse alone at home, perhaps in front of a mirror. A stopwatch is also useful as it allows the allotted time to be broken down into the various parts of the presentation. Memorize the beginnings and endings of main structural sections. The first serious rehearsal, preferably with the firm's managers who will attend the presentation, is often called the 'stagger through', probably because this is what it usually resembles. It is important to rehearse with appropriate managers because they will be able to ask the questions that will probably be raised by the customer or supplier.

Parts of the presentation will almost certainly need to be altered after this. The second rehearsal is called the run through, and this usually goes much more smoothly. Any last-minute amendments, such as the choice of a specific phrase or the alteration of visuals, can be made at this point. More than one run through is normally needed to become really comfortable with the material. It is a good rule that presenters should rehearse until they feel completely confident in what they are saying.

Taking questions

It will be virtually impossible to make a partnership presentation without taking questions. In any event, questions are desirable as they are evidence of interest, and are also useful in obtaining feedback. It is possible to structure the presentation so that questions are taken after each section.

The risk is that this will destroy the flow of the presentation or take up too much time. People usually prefer to ask questions as they arise and it is best to plan on this basis. When dealing with audience questions, there are a number of points worth remembering:

■ Thank the questioner for the question. This will reassure the questioner and others in the audience who might like to ask a question.

■ Listen hard. This will help ensure that the question is understood and will reassure the questioner.

■ If in any doubt, repeat the question. This will help other people to hear it and makes sure that you understand the questioner's meaning. If there is a genuine misunderstanding, the questioner will often correct the speaker by rephrasing the question.

■ After answering, check with the questioner that the answer is satisfactory.

■ Remind the audience whenever possible of the benefits in your partnership proposals. Answering questions is a good way to reinforce the key points by repetition.

■ Keep your answers short. The questioner will ask for more information if they really need it. Give examples whenever possible.

■ Answer to the whole audience. Begin by directly answering the person asking the question, then switch eye contact to other members of the audience.

■ Be tactful. Never get into an argument: you might be right, but you can't allow yourself to win.

■ If the answer is unclear or unknown, say so. Try to find out and let the questioner know later. If this is your intention, say so.

■ Hostile or difficult questions sometimes arise. Ask the questioner to repeat the question if you really need thinking time. This will occasionally lead to a genuinely different question being asked. Answer truthfully if the answer is known, or admit that you don't know and promise to find out. In such cases, the answer really must be discovered and fed back to the questioner.

■ This is also the best technique to use when faced with multiple questions in one. Quite often, the questioner does not really understand what it is he or she wants to know and asks a confused question. A request to repeat the question, perhaps tactfully pointing out that it seems to be more than one different question, is often the best tactic.

Most questions are genuine requests for help or for more information and should be viewed in this light. A partnership proposal is not to be taken lightly and must be accorded due consideration. Given this obvious background, a host of questions are bound to arise and it would be wise to prepare for these as part of the presentation planning, particularly during internal rehearsals.

Visual aids

'What is the use of a book,' thought Alice, 'without pictures or conversations?' (Lewis Carroll, *Alice's Adventures in Wonderland*).

There are many good reasons for using visual aids during presentations, though their use should be considered as part of the presentation plan. It is generally true to say that all presentations benefit from the thoughtful use of visuals of one kind or another, but the type to be employed will depend on a number of factors. The suitability of the venue is one, but the suitability of the occasion is far more important.

Most partnership presentations benefit from visuals, but 35mm slides, viewfoils and flipcharts or storyboards generally work best. The reason for this is simple: it is that the audience expects the presenter to describe a business opportunity, using materials to support the argument, not provide a cabaret. The benefits of good visuals will broadly be the same, whatever type is used:

■ A picture conveys a thousand words.
■ They save time on lengthy explanations. A bar chart can show the performance of various products under test against the same test last year far more easily than a verbal explanation.
■ They provide stimulus, bringing what might otherwise be a monologue to life.
■ They concentrate the attention of the entire audience on a single point of interest. This might be the key point of the presentation.
■ The audience is likely to remember vivid images.
■ They provide peaks of interest within the presentation, which helps to extend the audience's attention span. This is only the case if the visuals are clear, well thought out and full of impact.
■ Colour is an important memory stimulus, so visuals should be colourful as well as getting over important or complex points. Use colour for emphasis, but remember that colours such as orange and yellow reflect light and are more difficult to read from a distance than blue or black. Also, some people have difficulty in seeing red distinctly. Be sure that drawings and lettering are clear enough to be read from the back of the room.

Decide how many visuals are needed for the length of presentation you are planning. A good guide is not to use more than one every two minutes. Make sure that the message on your visuals reinforces what you are saying, is linked to your objectives and is kept simple. As a rule, don't use blow-ups of pages of type or columns of figures.

Choose the title of each visual carefully. The message must be at least partly conveyed through the name. Avoid using abbreviations in case no one else knows what they stand for. Keep titles simple, using only one idea, concept, message or structural element per visual. Most people will grasp simple points easily, even if they are part of something very complex. Use shapes whenever you can. We are all more likely to remember shapes, particularly if we can associate that shape with a particular colour and then link that to an idea.

Interpret where necessary, but only where necessary. Don't give a lengthy dissertation on the figures when they explain themselves adequately. If there is a lot of data, it would be wise to leave most of it out of the presentation, using only the most essential bits of information as visuals. Put the rest in a data book and hand it out separately.

Handling visuals can also be a delicate topic. Some of the people in the audience may be thinking about something else during some parts of the presentation. Don't distract them even further by showing visuals and continuing to speak as though nothing were showing.

Here are a few guidelines to help strike the right notes when using visuals:

■ Check the equipment to make sure that it works and is in focus. Make sure that everyone will be able to see the projector screen or flipchart.
■ Introduce each visual. It is being displayed to support a key point or to demonstrate something that is easier to see in a picture. Allow a moment for your words to sink in before showing the picture.
■ Show the picture and check that everyone can see. Avoid standing in someone's way. In a few words, explain what the key points are, then be quiet and let them take it in. Their body language will make it clear when to move on.
■ Focus attention on the speaker through your voice. The audience is here to see and listen to the presenter; the pretty pictures are only there to help.
■ When the audience has absorbed the point, remove the visual. If there is not another one to show right away, use a dark slide or logo slide or switch off the overhead projector. Never leave a visual on display for long periods; the light is distracting.
■ Use a pointer to illustrate and draw attention to the key points. When using an overhead projector, a pencil can be laid on the glass pointing at the part to be highlighted. Telescopic pointers are also available, as well as light pointers, although these can be very distracting in

inexperienced hands. Remember that all pointers can be distracting if misused.

■ When using video or audiotapes, make sure that the tape is wound to the point at which it should start. Check that the monitor is working and that the sound will not deafen everyone when the tape starts.

■ Use working models with care. They are wonderful when they work but can be an unmitigated disaster when they go wrong. The golden rule is to practise until perfect, and then have a standby model just in case.

■ Make sure that what is being illustrated is relevant. The points emphasized with visuals will be those that the audience remembers. They should be the main ones.

■ Talk to the audience – not to the visuals. It is bad manners for a presenter to stand with his or her back to the audience, but, much more importantly, it easily gives the impression that he or she has never seen the visuals before. It also makes it much more difficult for the audience to hear what is being said.

A typical partnership presentation

Supplier A, a manufacturer of steel trusses, RSJs and I-beams used in construction, wanted to turn Customer B, an existing customer in the construction industry, into a strategic partner. Its reasons for wanting to do so were partly defensive and partly offensive, but were in any case aimed at increasing and stabilizing profit while simultaneously opening up new profit opportunities for its intended partner.

Supplier A had done all the preparatory work, the customer had been contacted at managing director level and a meeting set up. Supplier A had an industry-wide problem in mind as an SPI, one that affected Customer B and every other major contractor. Of course, Supplier A did not know how to resolve this problem, and could not do so alone in any case. It did, however, have some carefully thought-out ideas concerning the problem, had researched it and believed that a partnership could be the way to solve it. A solution would provide a significant payoff for Customer B as well as having industry-wide implications for both partners. Even a partial solution would add serious sums to Customer B's bottom line.

At the meeting representing Customer B would be the managing director and finance director. The managing director and marketing director of Supplier A would make the partnership presentation. The two managing directors knew each other, though not well, but none of the others had met before.

The meeting

The Managing Director of Supplier A began by introducing the team and the subject matter. A description of the state of the construction industry, supported by a few viewfoils, was interspersed with some discussion on how the industry situation might develop. Supplier A then suggested that part of the industry's difficulty, a problem shared by Customer B, was the inability to get projects completed on time, thus incurring higher costs, delayed payments to subcontractors which forced some of them out of business and, in some cases, financial penalties. This, the managing director explained, was at the heart of the request for a meeting. The marketing director then took up the story.

The marketing director proposed to show a few viewfoils to help illustrate the case. The example used was a recently completed construction project in which Customer B had been the main contractor and Supplier A had been a key supplier. The marketing director showed a contribution statement for the project, explaining that it was the first time the firm had ever shown such financial information to a customer. It showed that Supplier A had made a positive contribution to overheads and profit by supplying Customer B, but a second table showed what might have occurred had the project run to time. The difference was significant.

The managing director of Supplier A asked if Customer B ever carried out similar financial appraisals. The finance director replied in the affirmative, but not on this particular project and not necessarily in this particular way.

Some discussion followed on the points raised so far. The marketing director then showed another slide suggesting three financial contribution scenarios for Customer B on the same project: good, medium and poor. The poor scenario showed the worst case on the project under discussion and the good scenario showed the best case. All three were extrapolated to show a similar effect for the combined total of projects undertaken by Customer B during the past 12 months. The sums were significant. Even the worst-case scenario would have added 3 per cent to Customer B's operating profit. The best case would have more than doubled this figure. Millions of pounds were at stake. The presenters asked if the customer had any plans to remedy this profit haemorrhage. The customer replied by asking what the supplier had in mind.

The marketing director said at once that the firm did not have all the answers to the problem of lost profit, but did have some ideas. Under the right circumstances, and with the right partner, the firm would be willing to develop these ideas, largely at its own expense, provided that any payoff was shared equitably. Some further discussion took place on what this might mean. Supplier A stated that any savings generated by such a programme should be shared on the following basis: in the first year, 60 per cent to Supplier A, in the second and subsequent years, 50/50. The marketing director added that the firm felt that 60 per cent share in the first partnership year was fair because it would have incurred most of the costs. 'Anyway', he added, '40 per cent of even £1 in extra profit would be more than you have now.'

Customer B asked how the supplier would go about finding and recovering what was agreed as being new profit. The managing director of Supplier A then proposed forming a study team, to be staffed jointly and to be financed entirely by the supplier, to investigate the problem and report back. 'What would this team look at?' was the customer's question. The marketing director replied that that should be agreed by discussion, but the initial idea was for the team to study the contractor's buying policy and ordering systems, stockholding policy and costs, onsite management and working practices, and organization of key subcontractors.

Customer B thought that this was a broad-ranging study and had three further questions relating to it. First, did the supplier believe that the necessary expertise existed within the two firms? Secondly, how would already busy people have the time to conduct the study? And thirdly, it was not sure what type or level of financial information would be sought, but would want to think this aspect over very carefully. The supplier replied that, if necessary, external experts would be hired at the supplier's expense and that most of the work would be carried out by the supplier's own staff who would be seconded to work part time on this special project. As far as access to financial data was concerned, the supplier recognized the sensitivity of this issue, but felt that it should not be allowed to stand in the way of what appeared to be a very worthwhile initiative. The study team would report back to both firms with recommendations on how the work and relevant part of the value chain could be reorganized, and the two firms would then agree to shake hands and walk away, or begin working on the proposals as partners.

'So your only commitment would be some management time during the study and your time to listen to the findings,' the managing director said. 'You would not be asked to commit yourselves to anything else until the team reported back, and only then once we had both agreed it was worthwhile.'

This would be the first stage in what could become a full-blown partnership, the marketing director continued. If the two firms liked working with one another and could see the benefits, a more formal arrangement might be entered into, perhaps in time even a legal contract in some form.

The customer wanted to know how long the study would take. 'Probably several weeks, but we can know that once we have decided exactly what they will do,' was the answer.

'Suppose we just take the recommendations proposed by the study team,' the customer said, 'and implement them ourselves. Why do we need to be involved in a partnership?'

'You can try to implement the recommendations alone,' the supplier replied, 'but some of them may be beyond your reach, stretching into the supply market for goods and services where we are the experts.'

'Why do we need a partnership at all?' asked the customer.

'Our knowledge is of the scale of the problem,' replied the supplier. 'Our assumption is that if you knew the answers to this problem, you would already have addressed it. Meanwhile, the lost profits continue.'

'We don't really see what's in this for you,' said the customer. 'Is it another way of selling us more RSJs?'

'Naturally, we want to sell more product,' the supplier's managing director replied, 'but we believe that the best way to do that is to work with a few selected customers to identify the best way, and that may not necessarily mean selling harder.'

Customer B's managing director said that the proposal was very interesting, but that no decision could be made today. Consideration would have to be given to whether this was seen as a more beneficial way of working, who might be involved in the study and what information could be released while it was being conducted.

Epilogue

Two weeks after the meeting, the managing director of Customer B called Supplier A and said that, in principle, the company was willing to commit to a trial study. A pre-study meeting was suggested to iron out some potential obstacles and clear the way.

This case demonstrates a typical partnership presentation structure and shows the type of question that arises. Among the most common customer questions, and some answers, are as follows:

Q Why would we want to enter into a partnership at all?

A There are benefits to be obtained within a partnership that are not available outside it. No sensible supplier would be willing to commit this scale of resource to a project entirely lacking in customer commitment.

Q If we did enter into a partnership, why you?

A We have a strategy to move from being ordinary suppliers to industry specialists and suppliers. We have studied the main industry issues, or those facing a particular customer, and believe we have some ideas that will work.

Q By partnership, do you mean a formal, legal contract?

A That would depend on how the two partners chose to work together. For the initiative being proposed now, something less formal should suffice.

Q What are the benefits of a partnership? Would these benefits accrue to us anyway?

A Potentially many. Higher or more stable profits, industry leadership, leading-edge working practices, access to new technologies and products not otherwise made available except on a normal buyer–seller basis, more harmonious relationships. No, the benefits would not accrue to the customer anyway. If this was so, why hadn't the customer already done the work alone?

Q What are the risks and can they be quantified?

A Very few, and yes. Since the partnership is designed to be bitten off in two chunks, and the first bite is the smaller, the risks for the customer are minimal. In fact, the only real risk is that the supplier abuses any inside knowledge gained. The probability of this happening is so remote as to be implausible. The main risk is borne by the supplier, who carries all or most of the first-stage cost.

Q Why should we divulge information to you that is private and confidential to our firm?

A To enable the technical and commercial study to progress properly. The customer will control what is released to the team at all stages of the study. The study will not look at the competitive situation, so no information will be needed on the customer's dealings with the supplier's competitors. Most of the information necessary will be verification of what could be assessed with reasonable accuracy in any event. This will be an information-sharing process, not one-way information giving. The supplier will divulge information as well.

Q What would happen once the work proposed for the partnership had been completed?

A Again, that would be up to the partners to decide. In all probability, other opportunities will be opened up on which the partners will want to continue working together.

Completing the partnership presentation successfully means being able to proceed to the next step in forming a strategic alliance, the technical and commercial study (Figure 7.1).

Technical and commercial study	Identify boundaries, scope and evaluate present practices	Internal consultancy

Figure 7.1 The strategic partnership model excerpt

The technical and commercial study

With the gaining of customer or supplier commitment following the partnership presentation, we have passed the second of three possible kill points in the building of a strategic partnership. The prospective partner, more than half way to becoming a real partner, can now be engaged at a different level. For the first time in the process, the firm can work with its selected supplier or customer in a way that will form the basis of future work together.

As we shall see in this chapter, structures and processes will be laid down that will not only assist in the work itself, but will also be the beginning of the growth of trust and mutual respect. The technical and commercial study will be followed by its evaluation and, in the vast majority of cases, this evaluation and what flows from it create the cornerstone of the future partnership. In this chapter, we will examine the study and its follow-up assessment, as well as describing the guidelines for the second partnership presentation.

It is important to note two issues at this stage. First, while all partnership projects incorporate this study, the weight of emphasis of the two aspects of technical and commercial undertaken by the same firm, or firms in different industries, can be dramatically different. To some extent, this will be dictated by the nature of the industry in which the two prospective partners operate. However, this is not the only factor to consider. One study may rest heavily on the need to explore and understand highly technical matters, while another may hinge on the ability to capture and exploit commercial data.

Secondly, it is essential that the scope and timing of the study be agreed with the supplier or customer before it begins. To miss out this step means going into the study with no clear remit and unclear objectives. It may not always be possible to determine the study scope in advance of making the first partnership presentation, but in these cases it must be agreed between the presentation and the start of the study, because it forms the basis on which the other party is being asked to make a commitment.

As well as the two aspects of the technical and the commercial, there are a number of other facets to a study, each of which merits some explanation. The facets to be discussed are: who will be involved, how the two sides will begin working with one another, how information will be transferred, how the study is to be evaluated, and the method to be adopted for making recommendations about the future organization of the partnership itself.

It is normal for both sides to enter into a partnership with hidden agendas, matters that are not disclosed to their partner, perhaps not at first, or ever. This is perfectly acceptable, even desirable, and to pretend otherwise is to ignore the realities of human relationships and business life. We cannot examine the hidden agendas of potential partners for the firm, but we can, and will, look at some of the items typically to be found on the proposing firm's agenda.

The study team

The composition of the core study team must be agreed with the prospective partner before it is formed. Indeed, it forms part of the commitment by the prospect that one or more people will be assigned to help with the study work. The core team may comprise anywhere between three and ten people, depending on the circumstances, with others joining the team as specialists, perhaps just for a few hours. The nucleus will be formed from the firm's internal consultancy, the same people who have undertaken much of the partnership-building work to date.

There should be a team leader, preferably a member of the proposing firm's staff, an expense budget and a place to work with the necessary support materials. The budget will, in virtually every case, be supplied and managed by the firm. The place of work will be the premises, often more than one, of the target customer or supplier. However, this does not preclude there being a separate location where the team can meet, and this can be anywhere, including hotel rooms. Modern portable PCs and other electronic communication tools make this a fairly straightforward task. Finally, outsiders such as consultants can be used, either to guide the firm through the process or to provide specialist technical or commercial support not available within either of the two firms involved in the study.

The first task of the study team is to schedule the work to be carried out, a subject that will shortly be dealt with in more detail.

Getting to know one another

The members of the study team may not have worked together before, even if they are all from the same part of the firm, and it is even less likely that they will have worked with the supplier's or customer's staff in this way. But this is only half the picture. The two firms concerned must get to know one another on a broader and deeper scale and that takes time, patience and skill.

Since technical and commercial studies vary so much, we will look at two examples taken from different industry situations. The first is a study carried out by a manufacturer of gas turbines which are installed in power-generating plants. The customer is a power-generating firm which sells the power produced to business and individual customers. The emphasis of the study is on technical matters. The other study is for a manufacturer of video and audiocassette tapes, supplied mainly to retail markets. The customer in this case is a multiple music retailer and the emphasis is on the commercial aspects of a partnership. The names used are fictitious in each case.

Powerpax

Powerpax is an internationally renowned manufacturer of gas turbines for power stations. Technical sales engineers examine blueprints and specifications for proposed new power-generating stations on a global basis and offer a contract to build, install and commission new plants, subcontracting much of the work to specialist firms. In addition, Powerpax will train customer and other suppliers' staff before, during and after installation as well as supplying a wide range of consumable products used in power generation. The firm offers what is known as a full service contract.

In recent years, Japanese competitors have begun offering a 'cherry picking' product. The customer may purchase the turbines from the Japanese producer and then choose to contract separately from anyone for the building, as well as the training and support work considered vital by everyone in the industry. This has the apparent advantage of lower cost, though the extent to which this is true is questionable.

Customer

The Northern Generating Authority, a major supplier of power to business and domestic customers, plans to build a new power station in its area. It will be gas powered. NGA is partly government owned. There are several potential worldwide suppliers, with some of which NGA has worked previously. It approaches two of them to hold preliminary discussions on possible design features, one of which is Powerpax. It also calls in a potentially new Japanese supplier, which has a reputation for no frills, good quality and lower build and installation costs.

Typically, all tender preparation work will be done by the generator before contacting potential suppliers so that the two sides have a basis for discussion. Powerpax knows that the Japanese supplier can undercut its prices by as much as 30 per cent and that it has already lost some purchase decisions, especially where government intervention can mean accepting the lowest bid.

Partnership

Powerpax considers a partnership approach suitable and had already earmarked NGA as a potential partner. As soon as preliminary discussions begin, it proposes working together in this new way. Several meetings take place, following which NGA agrees to put other contractors 'on hold' until a technical and commercial study has been completed.

The SPI – the basis of the study – was to be 'generating cost per unit of energy produced'. It was widely held that the industry was not particularly good at managing its prime cost. If NGA could reduce this cost, even by a tiny amount, the impact would be tremendous. During discussions, Powerpax suggested that possible cost-reduction areas were existing design and commissioning procedures, themselves based on the customer's buying policies, current working practices, and the design and supply of consumable products used in the power-generating process.

It was agreed that a team would be formed to study the issues and that this team would report to both boards in eight weeks. NGA proposed that Powerpax sign a confidentiality agreement forbidding the disclosure to a third party of any information gained during the study. This was also agreed. Following the study report, the two sides would either sign a partnership contract or continue to work together as before.

Study

A study team was established consisting of a nucleus of six people, two technical experts and a financial manager from Powerpax, and two people from NGA, one of whom was technical, the other representing purchasing. The sixth member was an external consultant employed by Powerpax to guide the study team through the process. A number of other specialists were identified during planning, some of whom would be needed more or less throughout the study, others coming in on a day-to-day basis.

The study was to be funded entirely by Powerpax, but an understanding was reached that if it were to lead to a full partnership, all savings would be split on the following basis: in year 1, 60 per cent to Powerpax, in year 2, 55 per cent to Powerpax, and in year 3, 50 per cent to Powerpax. A new agreement would be needed after that.

The work was divided into three parts: purchasing and design, commissioning and training, and consumable supplies from all sources. Overlaid on these three parts, all significant costs were to be examined by dividing them into direct and indirect costs. Each part would be subdivided into data gathering, analysis and interpretation and, finally, deciding what to recommend. Data gathering would be started in all three parts of the study at once and data interpretation would also be done together.

Recommendations would be left until all other work had been finished, but should quantify the profit impact as closely as possible. Final profit impact assessments would be made by both firms privately.

The work was planned to take 120 work days spread over the eight weeks of the study. Included in the first part – purchasing and design – would be the time taken and costs incurred by a power generator in getting an indicative tender prepared and, once potential suppliers were called in, the supplier's costs in responding to the tender, including design changes, the organization of the respective sales and purchasing departments, and possible new ways to structure these components in future, with benefits being quantified wherever possible. The second part – commissioning and training – would address the time period between the order being placed and the finished prod-uct being installed and commissioning trials beginning. It would include cus-tomer and other supplier staff training as well as current NGA work practices. Part three – consumable supplies – was considered the trickiest, because the study work would inevitably cover consumables supplied by Powerpax's com-petitors. To resolve this, it was agreed that only some consumables would be included, with NGA filling in the missing numbers afterwards.

Report

The presentation structure was to be divided into three sections: what work was undertaken; what was discovered; and what, if anything, was to be rec-ommended. It was planned that the first part could be covered in less than 10 minutes, part two in about 40 minutes and part three in about 20 minutes. A number of simulations were included in the second part of the presentation, showing the actual effects of current practice and the probable effects of new practice. Both were expressed as profit impacts. Time would be available after-wards for more discussion.

The presentation would be made to directors on both sides, who would then consider any action at a later date, and was made by members representing both firms. Several tables and charts would be used during the presentation and would show various costs and their current profit impact, as well as future scenarios. Three key charts to be shown at the end demonstrate how NGA, working in partnership with Powerpax, could reduce cost per unit of energy produced in a series of steps taken in each of the proposed three-year agree-ment. All figures are in US dollars. In the first year, NGA could save 0.71 cents per unit of energy produced, an additional 0.54 cents per unit could follow in the second year, and by the end of the third year another 1.20 cents could be found. This would make total savings over three years 2.45 cents per unit. To put this figure into context, NGA planned to generate 610 million units every month from its new station.

Outcome

Three weeks after the study presentation, the two sides agreed to enter into a formal partnership. A contract was drawn up and was signed by both parties.

Several of the study team's recommendations were rejected, some on either side, but over 90 per cent were accepted.

The SPI team currently working inside the partnership – the successor to the study team – is now working on phase two and the contract is in its fifth year. Savings made in the first year of the original partnership were 1.4 cents per unit, in year 2 they were 0.60 cents per unit, and in year 3 another 0.82 cents. In the process, and using similar power stations elsewhere as a benchmark, Powerpax increased its operating margin on this type of generating station from an average of 24.5 to 27.6 per cent over three years. Both sides found new ways of working together, many not envisaged in the original study, and new sources of profitability.

T-Tape

T-Tape is one of the world's largest manufacturers of audio and videocassette tape. It supplies other manufacturers with coated tape ready for putting into plastic cassette housings, as well as supplying blank (unrecorded) tape to consumer and professional markets on five continents. Tape is a highly competitive market where very little real differentiation exists between competing suppliers. Retailer purchase decisions are made on the reputation of supplier, product quality and price, though not always in that order. Consumer purchase decisions are usually driven by brand recognition, price and availability.

In the country in question, the consumer market for blank audiocassettes had been declining slowly and that for blank videocassette was static. These factors intensified competition. Margins on both class of product are thin for manufacturers, and retailers are unsure whether to remain in the product-market due to price-based competition from indirect competitors like newsagents and service stations.

Customer

Music Universe (MU) is a leading retailer, offering recorded CDs, audio and videocassettes and software. The chain also sells blank audio and video-cassette tapes. Its strategy was to offer consumers choice, the chance to try the product in store, always to have the latest products in stock and competitive prices. MU competes with similar stores offering similar merchandise, but in the blank tape market also with filling stations, newspaper stores and many others. This situation coloured its thinking about the blank tape market, which it saw as a market to withdraw from sooner or later.

T-Tape was one of MU's three blank videocassette suppliers, one of which supplied the chain's own brand, and one of four audiocassette suppliers. The share of tape supplied by T-Tape went up and down according to the offers made available to MU from other suppliers.

Partnership

T-Tape proposed forming a study team to examine two issues. First, could the market for blank tape be expanded, even by a small amount? (A 1 per cent increase in market volume would be worth $30 million.) And secondly, how could retailers in the music market better organize the switchover from old to new technologies? This latter point was considered to be an industry-wide problem because it caused retailers problems in managing inventory at times of changeover. These problems were often pushed back to suppliers, widening the difficulties. Both sides recognized that there were tremendous difficulties in tackling these issues, particularly the former, but that the payoff would be significant in the event of success.

After some discussion at board level, MU agreed to the study on the basis that it would be 100 per cent funded by T-Tape. Since making savings was not the object, this topic did not arise. However, T-Tape made it clear during its presentation that it hoped that MU could increase its share while simultaneously growing the market, and that T-Tape would be in an identical position with regard to its customer. In addition, it proposed that, since promotional activity was to be one of the central issues examined, activity between the two firms should be temporarily suspended while the study was in progress. This, it added, would help offset the cost of the work. A report would follow in about three months, and the two parties would decide on a course of action after that. MU calculated that since virtually all the cost was to be borne by T-Tape, and that there was no risk to itself, agreeing to a study was a safe thing to do. Any success meant all reward for no risk. Balancing these factors made it a simple decision to commit to supplying personnel and attending another meeting in three months.

Study

A small team of five people was formed, three from T-Tape and one from MU. The fifth member was a recently retired director of a credible and respected industry association, known to both parties and recruited for the duration of the study. The team met twice in quick succession, with the purpose of their first meeting being to receive training in team problem-solving methodology.

On the second occasion the team created a work schedule. The two questions would be treated separately, even though some members felt that there might be a link between them. They decided to take the first issue and look at merchandising and display, pricing, packaging and linked promotions. The emphasis would be on the first and last of these.

A specialist market-research agency was briefed to investigate consumer attitudes to instore displays of blank tape and to explore the factors thought to prompt the different types of occasion when blank tape was used. Meanwhile, two of the team members, working with an external agency used by MU, carried out a small but detailed study of all the consumer promotions that could be found in three different countries. Their task was to look specifically for promotions where blank tape had been linked to something else: other products, not necessarily in the music field, personalities and events. Simultaneously, a team member researched, mainly from data held by the two firms, how price points among different brands and different retailers had moved over a 12-month period.

Six weeks into the study the research agency reported its findings on consumer attitudes to instore displays and usage occasions. This prompted the team to commence its investigation into the second issue, even though the first part of the study was incomplete. The team believed that part of the switchover from old to new technologies instore was related to the way in which blank tape was merchandised during the introduction of new technologies. It determined to launch a specific investigation into this topic.

Report

Three months or so after the original meeting of board members, the study team reported its findings and recommendations. These were that the blank tape market could be expanded, but that only a small increase of between 1 and 2 per cent would be possible over a two-year period, though even this would entail significant increases to direct marketing costs. However, this meant the possibility of increasing market value at steady prices by between $30 and $60 million. Since MU had just over 10 per cent of blank videocassette volume in this market, the implications were clear. On the second issue, the team stated its belief that MU could organize the consumer switch from one technology to another more effectively and with less inventory cost and writeoff. New working practices would be needed to bring this about. Achieving this would also help T-Tape manage its manufacturing planning more efficiently as well as reducing the risk of packaging writeoffs.

Recommendations on the first question, increasing market volume, related principally to changing packaging materials and display formats to link videocassettes to new television broadcasts of motion pictures, concerts and sporting events, coupled with better targeting of heavy blank tape users. It was also recommended that pricing could be changed according to different seasons. Recommendations concerning the second issue also hinged on display formats, but not on packaging. A critical point made was that both parties would need to become more flexible, attuning business practice more to levels of consumer interest and demand.

Outcome

A partnership was agreed. There was to be no formal contract, but an agreement between the two firms to work closely on the study findings. No specific timescale was laid down for the various actions agreed, other than that all the work should be completed inside two years. The two firms would work more closely together than before and T-Tape has since become MU's favoured supplier of blank tape. It has also increased its share of business with MU.

The benefits accruing to MU are that it has sharply increased its share of blank videotape and has helped the overall market to grow slightly. It has also started to rethink accepted merchandising techniques and practice and has been in the forefront of new, instore design features. It now regards T-Tape as its favoured supplier because 'you help us make more money than our other tape suppliers'.

These are two examples of successful alliance approaches. Of course, not everyone is successful. But this is equally true of any other business strategy and experiences with proper analysis and evaluation make for steady improvement in the success rate.

Guidelines for technical and commercial studies

As has been stated already, studies are so diverse that a common, universally applicable list is impossible to construct. What is possible, however, is to offer some general guidelines that should apply to every study. These can be added to as circumstances dictate. Most of these general guidelines should be used during the planning phase.

- Agree at board level the outline, though not necessarily the detail, of work to be undertaken during the study. This must be done in advance of the study commencing to avoid introducing new topics once it has started. The schedule detail can be planned by the team after the study has begun.
- Prepare an outline plan of the work to be undertaken, showing which departments or functions will be involved and, even if in approximate terms, the level of their involvement. Agree this with the partner before commencing the study.
- Agree on those who will form the core team and who will be team leader. This should be a member of the firm's internal consultancy wherever possible. The core team can co-opt others as the study develops, obtaining the necessary approvals in advance. Try to select members who are skilled in rapport building and influencing skills. Some training in this field can be worthwhile.
- Decide how, how often and with whom the team will communicate during the study. Using common reporting tools will generally help. What the team should do if it runs into a problem it cannot resolve should also be taken into account at the planning stage.

■ Access to information must be clarified before starting the study. Both parties should know what information is to be available to the other side and what will not be. This is a vital point: more bad feeling can be created on this issue than any other, and too much will torpedo the study. Access to customer information that is considered sensitive should be obtained through the customer's own team member, who can always refer the question up the line in case of doubt.

■ Decide on the budget, which must be managed on the basis of who pays. If the proposing firm puts up all the expenses, it should determine how the budget is to be managed. The key criterion is to apply the budget to the topics agreed between the two firms. Any increase in the budget must be approved by the sponsoring executive in the proposing firm, but should also be communicated to the other party.

■ If the study runs into serious difficulties and seems unlikely to meet its objectives, say so. There is no point in continuing to waste money and time trying to force a square peg into a round hole. Openness is a key ingredient of successful partnerships. Opacity and bungled compromises are not.

■ Maintain steady communication at board level during the study. Part of the process is to build respect and trust, and this is helped by good communication. A telephone call once a week is usually all that is needed.

■ Aim to create a sense of urgency from the start. Studies usually involve people who are expected to do their normal work as well, and postponements on what seems to one person a relatively minor point can easily sabotage the entire timetable, causing everyone to lose interest or confidence.

■ Avoid taking on studies or specific tasks when the capacity to perform the task to a professional standard is lacking. It would be better to postpone the study or hire an expert to help with a specific task.

■ Be sufficiently flexible to allow for the airing of new ideas, even if it means changing the study in some way. Agree any proposed change with the other party before making it, explaining why it is necessary and how it will alter the intended outcome.

Completion of the technical and commercial study will lead to analysis and assessment of what has been learned (Figure 8.1). In part, this will reinforce what was already known or believed, but in other cases new information will come to light. The same team as conducted the study should make the evaluation and, having finalized this, should now prepare for the second partnership presentation. There are two significant differences between the first presentation and this one:

1 The second presentation is based on a commitment made earlier by the customer.
2 It should involve one or more members of the customer's own staff.

Evaluate study and form proposal	Identify wealth creation and propose best practice with business simulations	Internal consultancy

Figure 8.1 The strategic partnership model excerpt

Guidelines for study presentations

Although the emphasis is firmly on the study itself, many pieces of high-quality work have been known to fail because of a lack of skill in putting ideas and proposals over to others. The previous chapter covered this subject in some detail, but a few additional thoughts may help which apply specifically to presentations made after a technical and commercial study or during a full partnership.

- Always involve the other party in the presentation. It is not only more polite but, more importantly, it is more credible.
- Agree the content and recommendations in advance with all core team members and, separately, the sponsoring executive in the firm. First, this avoids someone saying that they disagree with something during the presentation, although this is not important if it is a trivial point. Secondly, it ensures that nothing will be proposed that has not first been approved at board level. And thirdly, it enables the executives receiving the proposal to be 'warmed up' by their own team member before attending the meeting. This is a good approach, since it gives people time to consider the issues 'in principle' before they hear them in detail.
- Use both firms' branding on all materials used, for example on overheads and report binders.
- Never agree to the delivery of benefits contained in study recommendations without proper commitment from the other side. That is not a true strategic partnership, nor will it ever lead to one.
- If possible, try to agree a date by which the party receiving the partnership proposal will respond.

The second partnership presentation is the third kill point in the building process. It is possible that, having considered the study report and proposals, the prospective partners agree not to go any further. In such cases, the proposing firm will have incurred costs that it is unlikely to be able to recover, but will almost certainly have strengthened its relationship with the supplier or customer concerned. Being realistic, suppliers are much less likely to turn down this kind of approach; the risk, such as it is, exists virtually entirely on the customer's side of the equation. It is a risk nonetheless, but business consists of taking calculated risks.

In the two cases described above, the financial risk was borne by the firm proposing the partnership, in both instances to a customer. This is the reality on most occasions, but there are some instances where the customer will agree to share the burden. It depends on the circumstances and the judgement made as to the balance between incurred cost and potential reward.

In the majority of cases, and having reached this point in the process, the two firms will usually agree to form a partnership. Failure to do so at this stage probably means that one of the following has occurred:

- The proposing firm has made a mistake in identifying the SPI. This is unlikely to occur in practice, because the SPI will have been agreed by both sides during the initial presentation and discussion that followed it, leading to mutual commitment.
- The proposing firm has given too much away in the presentation, creating the impression in the mind of the customer that everything can be achieved alone, without the need for the proposing firm as a partner. This can be caused by failure in planning the presentation structure or by the design of the technical and commercial study. Customer or supplier staff will be involved in the study and therefore will see most of what it generates. They are bound to feed this back to their own management, and so the process of producing and communicating data as well as recommendations needs to be managed.
- The proposing firm has said too little of substance in the study presentation, giving the impression that the partnership goals would be too difficult for anyone to attain. This may be true; if it is, say so. However, it is more likely to have been caused by inappropriate structuring of the presentation, with too little weight being laid on the recommendations and how they might be implemented.
- The firm receiving the proposal feels that the chemistry between the two firms is not right. This would probably have surfaced by now and would have caused the firm receiving the proposal to turn it down at the first meeting.
- The study itself failed to show that the benefits were worth the effort required to reach them. This could be the result of an inappropriate SPI or a prospective partner not fully committed to the partnership concept. It could also be true, in which case the proposal should be abandoned.
- One prospective partner does not have the resources to undertake or complete the work. This possibility should have been eliminated much earlier during the customer selection step. However, it might be that the partnership programme should be scaled back in order to mesh existing resources more closely with opportunities, or that new

resources should be sought, or that the programme should be phased over a longer period.

It is important to stress that where the partnership goes forward, all future costs and rewards are shared on a basis to be agreed between the partners. This can vary from time to time even in the same partnership. For example, the two firms may agree to split the costs of one particular project undertaken within the partnership on the basis of the supplier picking up 75 per cent of the cost, while at the same time the costs of another project will be shared 50/50. In both instances, the sharing of rewards should be commensurate with the sharing of costs. This is another commitment, building on and reinforcing earlier ones.

At the end of this second partnership presentation, another, more complete commitment should be obtained from the customer or supplier. In part, this is to take the former members of the study team and, where necessary, amend their numbers or composition to form a new and permanent team who will see through the programme of work. Throughout the book this is referred to as the SPI team, but any other working title preferred by both partners can be used. Secondly, the commitment of cost referred to above should be made. And thirdly, the commitment to work in a new type of business relationship for a common good is central to bonding the partnership together. It is the sum of these three commitments that marks a beginning of a true strategic partnership. Failure to obtain the necessary commitment at this point, though unusual, should kill off the initiative (Figure 8.2).

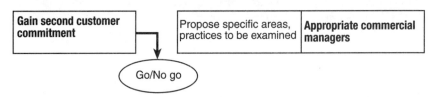

Figure 8.2 The strategic partnership model excerpt

Gaining these commitments enables the two firms to begin the work that has been the focus of so much energy (Figure 8.3).

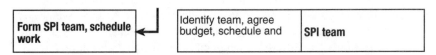

Figure 8.3 The strategic partnership model excerpt

The SPI team approach

There are two critical issues that have to be considered in getting organized to carry through the programme of work agreed at or after the second partnership presentation. The first is getting started with the partnership team, known here as the SPI team, and its vital supporting mechanisms. And the second is planning and executing the work itself. Both these topics will be covered in this chapter, together with a number of relevant matters, including where the team should be based, its operating guidelines, problem solving, communication systems and reporting methods, and arbitration procedure.

Forming an SPI team

The formation of an SPI team will depend on several factors. The most important of these is that the firm will very probably choose people from within its existing personnel, rather than trying to recruit people from outside specifically for the purpose. That said, there is no reason that the leader of the team should be someone expressly from the sales or marketing function. It does not matter which part of the firm team leaders come from, so long as they are selecting according to the right criteria. These can be divided into what we might call natural abilities and acquired skills.

In the first case, the main criteria that should be met by all team leader candidates are these:

- *Clarity*. The ability to express clearly goals and strategies, problems and opportunities is a salient feature of good leaders. People rally, not to charismatic leaders, who are so rare in any case, but to those who are able to express group aims clearly and in a way that attracts the support of a majority.
- *Integrity*. The person chosen must command the respect of others and, to do so, must demonstrate this elusive ideal. Perhaps 'weight' is a better word, though not in the hierarchical sense, since most people seem to know the difference between heavyweights and lightweights. 'Strength of character' is probably an even better term. People with integrity hold strongly, occasionally too inflexibly, to positive personal principles; this is apparent, and usually appealing, to others. People with integrity 'stand for something' and everyone else recognizes what it is.

■ *Optimism*. This is meant not in the generally accepted sense of the word, but in relation to 'people who like people'. People who like others as a basic outlook on life and enjoy collaborating with them, without necessarily being gregarious, tend to have the natural abilities necessary to steer teams through thick and thin, key among which is a positive, 'can do' attitude.

■ *Determination*. Single-mindedness is, perhaps, another way of expressing this ability. Carried too far it becomes stubbornness, but determined people usually get things done. Decisiveness also seems to be a running mate of determination, so that where we find one, we find the other.

Under the heading of acquired skills, those most important in an SPI team leader are these:

■ *Organization*. The ability to organize a group of people engaged on a set of disparate tasks, often in different parts of the partnership and sometimes reporting elsewhere, is a key skill. The organization of the work itself also calls for the highest level of skills.

■ *Negotiation*. All work is a negotiation and partnership work is no different. But here, the team leader and, to some extent, team members must negotiate in three functional places. Negotiation occurs within the team and with both partners, sometimes simultaneously.

■ *Delegation*. There is only so much that anyone can do well, but some people try to do everything and finish up managing beneath their proper level of authority – in other words, doing someone else's work for them. This is not only poor use of resources, it risks turning off everyone else in the team.

■ *Mentoring*. Team leaders must have the personal motivation to teach, train and coach other people, while at the same time achieving the aims of the partnership. This means that they must be both task and people oriented.

The functional skills that the team leader brings, whether from human resources, finance, marketing or elsewhere, will complement the natural abilities and acquired skills referred to above.

The remainder of the team will be divided into various kinds of specialist, bringing the different sets of knowhow vital to achieve success. In any partnership, there will be a requirement for both technical and commercial specialists, though the weight of emphasis will be different in each and will vary from time to time as the programme of work assumes new characteristics.

In selecting members of an SPI team, it is important to begin with considering the needs of the other partner as well as of the work programme. For example, one member of the partnership may have an overriding need for supplier inputs to help manage physical distribution and inventory management. Recognizing this, a focused supplier, working in a partnership, will co-opt into the SPI team one or more experts in distribution logistics so as to harmonize, as far as possible, the efforts of the two firms in this important area. Another partnership may need to acquire new technologies fast as a means of shortening learning curves and reducing learning-acquisition costs. It would need one or more members in its team with expert knowledge in the programmes necessary to shift the desired new technology to the customer.

The following is obvious from the above discussion:

- Different SPI teams will have a different membership make-up, and this membership can only be determined once the layout of the work programme becomes clear.
- Membership can be for different periods of time, team leadership being the exception to this rule. Other members may come into the partnership to help with one particular piece of work and leave as soon as it has been completed. Others may stay for lengthy periods. The same applies to members supplied by the customer or supplier, although there are obvious benefits of having someone perform the 'anchor role' on behalf of the other partner.
- To repeat a point above, membership is a full-time job only for the team leader. Other members devote as much time to the partnership as is deemed necessary to complete the work. This must be balanced against the need for them to continue in their normal organizational roles. Clearly, this implies some reorganization of the firm's workload beyond the boundaries of a partnership, since in most cases people must be released from some part of their normal duties in order to undertake partnership work.
- Job descriptions, standards of performance and other internal documentation will need to be amended to take account of changed duties, responsibilities and accountabilities.

Three other issues are of prime importance in choosing team members. The first is that members must be team players, a point that covers both partners. There is no room for lone wolves in an SPI team. The second issue is related to a common organizational problem, that of 'cloning' – hiring or promoting people we consider to be like us. SPI teams need a variety of talents. No orchestra would sound very good if it were composed entirely of pianists. And thirdly, partnerships are an excellent way for people to learn new skills, ideas or techniques. The concept of 'on-the-job training' is never more real than when applied in the partnership context.

One other aspect of this approach can be important. More and more firms have adopted flattened organizational structures as a means of eliminating cost. This has usually meant a reduction of middle manage-ment layers where many career opportunities traditionally existed. Firms must now find other ways of satisfying the career aspirations of bright, ambitious people. SPI teams offer the opportunity to get people involved in a broader job context and role. Certainly, the role of team leader will be seen as a clear promotion in most cases, but the extent to which the role of other members is viewed as a promotion will vary from one firm to another, depending largely on the culture and prevailing circumstances.

A number of points should be noted in this respect:

■ The move does not have to be a hierarchical promotion to meet an individual's career needs, although it is possible to build this into a career plan if desired. It can, however, be seen as a diagonal step towards promotion.
■ Since the move is not permanent, it is possible for someone to opt out of an SPI team if they don't like the work or are unsuited to it.
■ The move helps broaden people's horizons and deepen understanding of the role performed by other functions of the business. This must be of benefit to the firm as a whole.
■ Secondment to an SPI team enables managers to see staff in another role without permanently switching their jobs, and so assess them for other responsibilities in the future.
■ The secondment will be viewed by the customer as a reinforcement of the firm's partnership commitment.
■ SPI teams are virtually unique in offering opportunities for staff to be seconded to suppliers and customers, and vice versa, within a business development framework. The principal difference between it and other schemes is that in a partnership, people are engaged on real work as distinct from merely learning about the role of the other party.

Training an SPI team

Training and developing people is a massive subject, and one that is beyond the scope of this book. That people do need training and devel-oping seems beyond doubt in most forward-thinking firms, but there is one subject to which the partners should give some serious thought: how teams should solve problems. One of the few certainties is that problems will arise in a partnership, just as certain in fact as that they will arise in any other type of enterprise. Problems occurring in the partnership con-text, however, take on a different hue. The subject should be viewed within the dimension of two different firms working together in a for-mal relationship and seen against the background of the two sets of procedures and dynamics at play. Molehills can easily become mountains and mountains can become immovable objects, refusing to allow the programme to develop properly. The end result can be stunted growth or partnerships cut off in their prime.

There are many systems for solving problems, but what is really important is that the one chosen is easy to apply and will cover most problems that an SPI team will run up against. We will look at two approaches, one logical and the other creative. Both can be used independently, or the creative approach can be applied to the results of the logical methodology. The two techniques are gap analysis and brainstorming.

Gap analysis

Gap analysis is a problem-solving method that lends itself to the special needs of team problem solving, in which some consensus is vital among so many different opinions. This is partly true in the general sense of business, of course, but here we are faced with the additional complexity of the involvement of people from two different firms, representing as they do two different cultures. In virtually any business situation, many day-to-day problems are dealt with instantly, on the spot. The difficulty arises when the second or subsequent problem occurs. The fact that one or more people solved the problem, and may do so again, is almost immaterial. What counts is that because no structured process was used, it is very hard to replicate, very difficult to learn and virtually impossible to teach anyone else.

Another difficulty with this type of rapid problem solving, for anything other than low-risk decisions, is that the real problem is incorrectly identified. Most people have found that a structured technique is better for dealing with anything other than run-of-the-mill matters, and it is on this type of methodology that we shall now concentrate.

A problem is recognized as existing when what should be happening does not happen. The planned and the actual become different because something has changed. Any search for the cause of the problem must therefore begin with a rigorous search for what has changed.

The model in Figure 9.1 illustrates how this approach works and is followed by a more detailed analysis of each step in the model. The process begins when one member of the team reports a problem. The team leader then convenes a meeting, asking the reporter of the problem to write a brief, one-paragraph definition of the problem, circulating it at the meeting.

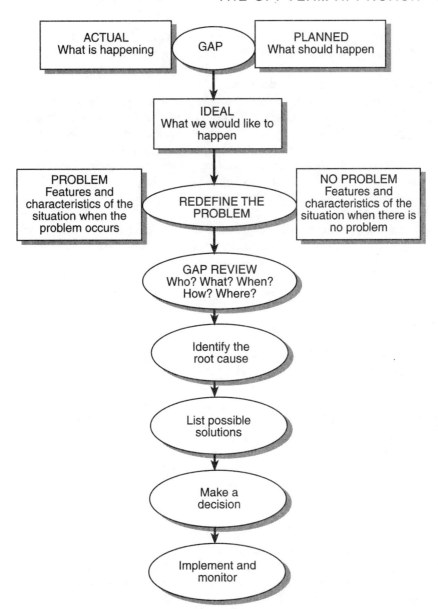

Figure 9.1 Gap analysis model

Step 1 – Define the problem

As has been indicated, there is a problem when what was supposed to happen did not happen, or where the actual outcome of a set of actions was different from what was intended. Begin by describing what did happen or the actual outcome. Once agreement has been reached on what happened, describe the ideal outcome. This may be different to what was originally planned, perhaps just because the original plan was made some time ago or because standards have since been raised.

Step 2 – Redefine the problem
The real problem must be defined as precisely as possible or the team risks solving the wrong one. More than one definition should be created, because the first one may be wrong – just ask several witnesses to the same accident what they saw. Several people should be asked to write a problem redefinition because problems always manifest themselves in different ways, depending mainly on hierarchical level and functional role. Redefinitions should always be written by people who are affected by the problem.

Stating the features and characteristics of the situation when the problem occurs and when it does not will help clarify the real problem. After the team has studied the various redefinitions, they must decide how the real problem is to be stated. Wherever possible, the problem should be quantified.

Step 3 – Carry out a gap review
This step is taken simultaneously with Step 2 and involves asking the following questions as they apply to the restated problem: Who? What? When? Where? How? Avoid asking 'why' too many times during this step, because it may lead to a false conclusion as to the root cause of the problem by focusing people's attention on the wrong part of the problem-solving process.

This step is essentially a reality check, but it also helps establish a boundary line around the problem that will be particularly helpful later in searching for differences to help develop possible causes. The team should now analyse the differences between the problem and no-problem situations.

Step 4 – Identify the most likely causes
To begin working on this step, don't focus too much on one possible cause, but try to create a list. Verify each one by testing them against the 'problem/no problem' descriptions obtained from the boxes shown alongside 'redefine the problem' and 'gap review' in Steps 2 and 3. From this testing will come the cause that best fits the description of the problem.

Keep two points in mind: first, that up to this stage in the process the team has not been looking for solutions or action; and secondly, that it is the root cause of the problem that must be found. Do not confuse peripheral causes with root causes: the former may be no more than symptoms of the real cause. The purpose of the four steps up to this point is simply to understand the problem in detail and to isolate the most likely cause of the problem. The team should agree on the root cause before moving on.

Step 5 – List all possible solutions

This is the stage at which all the possible courses of action should be listed and investigated. Many of these will have surfaced during the discussion up to this point, and it is a good idea to list them quickly on a flipchart before they are lost. However, the team must not dwell on possible solutions until reaching this step.

In some problems, there may be only one viable option available; in others there may be many. Before committing itself to action, the team should first examine whether there are alternative methods of implementing a solution and, if so, it should select the best one.

Step 6 – Make a decision

When a list of alternative solutions has been developed, a decision has to be made and implemented. This is the step where the pluses and minuses of each prospective solution are analysed by examining the consequences of each, assessing each one against planned outcomes, testing against the ideal and finally making a selection. A second reality check may be used here too, which is to ask how certain people or functions would react if the proposed solution were to be implemented. For example, how would the board members of both partners react?

Step 7 – Implement and monitor

Having been through all the previous steps, including making a decision as to which of the potential solutions to choose, it is vital that everyone concerned fully supports the chosen option and acts effectively to carry out the decision, monitoring, reviewing and modifying as necessary. All team members should support the decision, even if they do not fully agree with it. Earlier discussion provides ample opportunity for members to state opposing points of view. Team decision making means that members support decisions that have been properly arrived at.

Brainstorming

If gap analysis emphasizes a logical, rational methodology, brainstorming meets the creative needs of teams in problem solving. Brainstorming provides a formal setting for creative thinking and the subsequent generation of ideas. In itself it is not a technique, but a setting in which the normal constraints of everyday thinking can be suspended. In this context, there are three key guidelines for brainstorming:

■ *Suspend judgement.* Never evaluate the ideas being produced during the session, whether they are yours or other people's. Avoid using phrases such as: 'that won't work' or 'that's silly'. The objective of the exercise is to generate lots of ideas as quickly as possible, not to evaluate and criticize those that are put forward. That can come later.

■ *Let go and freewheel.* The informal setting of the brainstorming session is a way of saying 'anything goes' or 'the normal rules of thinking do not apply'. It is a time when people are not only allowed but encouraged to drift and dream and bring into play the subconscious mind. Do not be worried about putting forward what may appear to be wild or silly ideas – everyone should be suspending judgement.

■ *Leapfrog.* This is where the group comes in. Always be prepared to pick up somebody else's idea and suggest others stemming from it. It often happens that an idea may seem very obvious or trivial to one person and yet it can combine with other ideas in someone else's mind to produce something very original.

Two roles are key to the success of brainstorming, session leader and note taker. There are no hard and fast rules for the size of the group, but more than twelve and things begin to get unmanageable, fewer than five and there is a tendency for the session to become an argument about the relative merits of ideas. The session leader, who does not have to be the team leader, has an important role to play in guiding the session and stopping people from evaluating or criticizing the ideas of others too early. This is a cardinal sin in brainstorming. The session leader needs to ensure that not everyone speaks at once, and that everyone gets the opportunity to make a contribution. However, going round the table in circles for ideas from each person in turn or picking on people for ideas is to be avoided. The session leader should only ask an individual for a comment if the group has lost momentum for a moment, as this may help get the session moving again.

The session leader should make sure that the note taker is managing to keep up with the flow of ideas, which may be quite rapid, particularly in the early stages. Notes should be written on a flipchart, and it is best to have two flipcharts so that everyone can see them. It may be that some ideas will need to be restated so that the note taker can get them down. If this is the case, the person who came up with the idea should be asked whether it has been recorded correctly. At any stage, if someone feels that the note taker has incorrectly noted an idea, he or she should be asked to change it.

The session leader may be asked to rule whether an idea has already been put forward. Only if this is clearly the case should the latest idea be rejected. If there is any doubt, the idea should be noted. The group should be constantly reminded of the nature of the problem being brainstormed and brought back to the subject where necessary. This is easier said than done, in that the purpose of the exercise is to generate ideas and on the surface some of the ideas may appear to have little relevance to the problem under consideration. Individual flights of fancy should therefore be allowed, but any group divergence should be stopped. The session should be ended, either after a pre-determined time or if energy appears to be flagging, whichever is earlier.

Thirty minutes is quite long enough for most brainstorming sessions. It is a good idea for the time to be agreed beforehand and if interest appears to be dwindling the group should either be encouraged or the session brought to an end. There is no benefit in trying to squeeze the very last idea out of the group or allowing the session to go on for an indefinite amount of time.

Immediately the session is closed, and with everyone still present, the note taker should read back through the pages of notes with the aim of converting the many ideas into a permanent, legible record. The notes need to make sense, not just immediately but also in the future. The note taker should be prepared to read through the list at any time should the session leader or group members so wish.

The steps of a brainstorming session are simple and are described below.

Step 1 – Warm-up session
It is always a good idea to have a warm-up session, particularly if group members are not familiar with one another or the brainstorming process. This typically addresses some random issues on which everyone would have something to contribute, but which are unconnected with the problem to be worked on. For example, 'How to reduce peak hour traffic on motorways' or 'How to encourage people to use litter bins in the street more often'.

The idea of this session is to illustrate the type of ideas that may be offered and to show that evaluation is definitely not allowed, as well as to get the group in the right frame of mind. Fun should be the catchword at this stage. This session should last no more than 10 minutes.

Step 2 – State the problem
The problem owner should state the problem in detail, explaining it to the group. Brainstorming may be introduced as a session in gap analysis once the team has reached Step 2. Whether it is used or not, a brief discussion should now follow to ensure that everyone taking part has a clear understanding of the problem.

Step 3 – Restate the problem
Once the problem has been outlined, the group should be encouraged to stand back from it and attempt to see it from various angles. Their suggested restatements of the problem should be written on a flipchart for everyone to see, prefaced by the words 'How to...'. Some of the restatements will be very close to the original problem statement, while others may illuminate new facets.

In those cases where the problem is relatively clear cut, it may look the same from every angle and no restatements need to be considered. For more complex problems, there are likely to be many ways in which they may be viewed. It will be seen differently depending on the force of the impact it makes.

Step 4 – Select a restatement

When at least six restatements have been proposed, one, or perhaps two combined, should be selected for brainstorming and written on a fresh flipchart sheet. This should be prefaced by the words 'In how many ways...?'. For example: 'In how many ways can we reduce the cost of performing this task?'

Step 5 – Brainstorm the problem

Emphasize once more the guidelines of suspending judgement, letting go, freewheeling and leapfrogging. In addition, the group should be encouraged to go for quantity, and at certain stages it may be helpful to set a target at which it can aim.

Step 6 – Wildest idea

For a finale, the group should be asked to select what they consider to be the wildest idea among those suggested. This should be written on the flipchart and the group asked to generate ideas from it. A few minutes spent on this step can generate some really radical thinking which can then be applied during Step 7.

The team may need a break between Steps 5 and 6 and it is highly desirable to have one between Steps 6 and 7. This may be of a few minutes' or a few days' duration. The urgency of the situation will often dictate this.

Step 7 – Evaluation

Too many brainstorming sessions finish at either Step 5 or 6. While evaluation is to be avoided during the session, it is an essential step afterwards if anything useful is to be gained. In the evaluation session the ideas should be sifted to extract those that could be useful. The main tasks of the evaluation are:

- To determine ideas that are obviously helpful.
- To extract from ideas that are clearly wrong or ridiculous any kernel of an idea that may be applied to the problem in hand.
- To list functional ideas, new approaches to the problem, new aspects of the problem or any additional factors that have come up that should be taken into consideration. While none of these is an actual solution to the problem, they should nevertheless be recorded since they may well help in the final outcome.

■ To identify those ideas that can be tried out with relative ease, even though they may appear to be wrong at first sight.
■ To pick out those ideas that suggest that more information could be collected from certain areas.
■ To weed out those ideas that have already been tried.

At the end of the evaluation session there should be three lists:

■ Ideas that are immediately useful.
■ Areas for further exploration.
■ New approaches to the problem.

The evaluation session is not simply an opportunity to discard and criticize. Some creative effort should be brought to bear, and encouraged, in extracting usefulness from ideas before they are discarded or in spotting an idea that looks as if it ought to be discarded but that can, in fact, be developed into something beneficial.

There are two reasons for adopting a team problem-solving strategy: to solve problems and to signal commitment and professionalism to the other partner. There are two steps to this: the first is for the firm to learn the problem-solving process for itself; and the second is to pass the knowhow on to the customer or supplier's representatives by means of the SPI team.

The first SPI team meeting

Clearly, there will be an element of people getting to know one another at the first meeting. At one level this will be because people do not know one another. At another, more common level, it will be that people need time to get used to a particular style of working and a new situation. These factors should be borne in mind as the team leader convenes the first few meetings.

We will deal with the agenda shortly, first developing some other points of relevance. It is important to establish the ground rules in any team situation and, in this case, the most important are as follows:

■ *Clarify the team's objectives.* Eventually these will have to be stated in the work schedule, but that has not yet been created. For the present, the team leader should stress the importance of meeting deadlines and budgets. Most importantly, the overall objectives for which the SPI team has been created must be spelled out. As the work schedule is developed, the team leader will want to identify the relevant objectives for each constituent part and keep these in front of the team at all times.

■ *Establish criteria to measure team performance.* At the first meeting the SPI team leader should initiate a discussion aimed at agreeing what constitutes good performance, leading the team to develop some simple, measurable criteria. Measurement should then be made at regular intervals against these standards.

■ *Establish decision-making criteria.* People need to be clear on what decisions can be taken independently of the team, which are team consensus decisions, which are to be made by the team leader, and which are to be referred to someone outside the immediate team. In the latter case, the sponsoring executive on either side will be known in advance and so it will be clear where decisions referred outside the team are being sent. It is a fairly straightforward task to set this process out on one or two pages and circulate it at the first meeting.

■ *Develop reporting procedures.* It is important that the team is clear on what has to be reported, to whom and by when. The same reports should go to both firms; anything of a more sensitive nature will be fed back in any case. A critical point is to establish the importance of speedy and actionable information within the team and to others at all times.

■ *Begin scheduling the work.* Working from the outline or set of goals already established as a result of meetings and discussions between executives of the two firms concerned, the team should start planning the work schedule. This will include what must be done, planned start and finish dates, who will do the work, whether it can be done in parallel with anything else, and its intended outcome expressed in the form of an objective.

■ *Get the resources.* The resources necessary for the team to operate effectively must be put in place. This can include meeting space, administrative assistance, electronic communication tools, people time and money.

■ *Set the standards.* These should be written, minimum standards of performance and must be consistent for each team member as well as being consistent with the culture of both firms as far as possible.

■ *Determine team recognition.* This is part of the process of branding the partnership, especially within the client or supplier firm, as well as signalling a unified approach to everyone involved. Some visible means of identifying the team in action is desirable. A tie or tie pin, a hard hat, a lapel badge, a jacket, briefcases or other items of clothing or equipment may all be used to signal the arrival of the SPI team. What is more important than which item is selected is the fact that this is one of a number of signals being sent consistently to the partner, each one supporting the others in establishing a base of uniqueness.

Apart from the initial meetings, the SPI team will regularly be involved in other meetings. These will follow one of three formats:

- With members of the customer or supplier's staff where the work is being done. These will fall into two categories: when a member can visit someone belonging to the staff of the other partner alone; and when this is best done in tandem with the supplier or customer's team representative. The distinction is a largely subjective one, but important. There will be occasions when the team needs information or action that might be resented by the person of whom it is being asked, mainly because it is being requested by an outsider. The same request from a colleague, when it is known to be backed up by top management, has a different ring to it. These occasions will diminish over time.
- With team or other colleagues on a one-to-one basis.
- When the team meets formally as a group. Most meetings of the latter type should be conducted during the lunch hour. The two reasons for this are, first, that team members have their normal duties to accomplish and may only be available for short periods at certain times, and secondly, that one-hour meetings force the meeting leader and other team members to concentrate on the important points.

The team leader should use an agenda to call a meeting, appending a few words to each of the topics to be discussed. The topic list itself should be generated by the team leader's asking each member to be present what they feel should be included. Remember that while meetings are essential, they are also considered one of the great wastes of organisational time. This is due to several reasons:

- Poor agenda planning, resulting in too much time being spent on some subjects and not enough on others.
- People being present who have no need to be there, or sometimes no need to be there for the whole meeting.
- Poor meeting control, either as a result of poor meeting leadership or a poorly structured agenda.
- They are not decision focused. Many, perhaps the majority, of business meetings are for the purpose of reaching decisions. Yet this often fails to happen, leaving people feeling frustrated with the meeting leader as well as the whole process of meetings. The meeting sometimes has to be reconvened in order to reach a decision that should have been taken at the first one. An equally bad alternative is that the team leader will take decisions after the meeting has ended, leaving everyone else wondering why a meeting took place at all.

As well as the date, time and place of the meeting, an agenda should specify what is to be discussed – and therefore, what will not be – giving a brief explanation against each topic of any necessary background, the approximate amount of time to be given to each topic, who will introduce the topic and whether it is intended that a decision should be reached. If anyone is to research specific points in advance of the meeting, this should be noted on the agenda.

27 July, 1230–1400. Meeting room 2
Sandwiches and refreshments provided

No.	Topic	Time	Decision
1	Progress report. Progress reports on projects C, D & F. All members. JL to bring latest test data from trials on project D. PH to update team on availability of financial data for all three projects.	60 mins	Not required
2	Agency briefing. Agency to brief team on readiness of presentation materials for projects A & B. This presentation is scheduled for 11 August in the boardroom.	20 mins	Yes, we must agree presentation aids at this meeting
3	Help! Request from BK to provide technical data for product Y. Do we have this? Can we get it?	10 mins	Yes, once action is known

Figure 9.2 Example SPI team meeting agenda

There is no space allocation in the example in Figure 9.2 for 'any other business'. In fact, it is covered under item 3. When the team leader called each member, the question was raised as to whether there were any specific items, in addition to 1 and 2, that members wanted to discuss.

Instead of having minutes typed and circulated after meetings, which takes too long and ties up secretarial support, use a format like the one shown in Figure 9.3 for team communications. It is normally sufficient for these to be written by hand during the meeting – the task can be rotated among members – as long as the writing is legible. The handwritten pages are then photocopied and circulated to each member immediately. Each reviews the action points as soon afterwards as possible, highlighting any points to which attention must be given. The form is then used as the agenda for further discussion at the next team meeting. Another method is to use electronic means. In practice, the two can easily be combined by setting up a page on appropriate software, typing action points as the meeting reaches conclusions, and transferring the data to other PCs or portables as soon as the meeting finishes.

No.	Action to be taken	By whom	By when
1	Incorporate new financial data provided by PH into projects C, D & F and report new data back to PH	JL, AR & GH	6 August
2	Finance to provide new costings based on data received from other team members	PH	15 August

Figure 9.3 Example layout for meeting action points

The SPI team will be based where most or all of the work will be conducted. This will be at the premises of the supplier or customer in question, and may include factories, warehouses and offices. Although much of the work will be carried out in situ, by working with people in their offices or production locations as well as at the firm's own premises, the team must have secure space in which to meet and work privately. This means there is a need to allocate office space at the customer's or supplier's site.

Ideally, the space should be large enough to house the team meeting, assuming that everyone attends. If this is not possible for some reason, meetings will have to take place at another, possibly external, location. A working space for purposes other than meetings is essential, however, and should be raised at the time of, or immediately after, the second partnership presentation.

The question of charging office accommodation to the SPI team is occasionally raised. There is no hard-and-fast rule here, only that the team has to work within its budgetary constraints and, if some expense is incurred for an office, then it has to be deducted from somewhere else in order to pay for it.

The next item to tick off is furniture and equipment. Normally, office furniture – chairs, desks and so on – will be provided at the same time as the office in which it is sited. Equipment is a rather different matter. Equipment such as photocopiers tends to be sited where groups of people have access to it and this rule is most likely to apply to an SPI team too.

Computers, including portables, are best provided by the firm, along with the software that runs on them. This raises the important question of security. Care must be taken, as in every commercial situation, to guard valuable data. The difference here, of course, is that the firm will be transmitting data received from the other partner, either to other networked PCs or to a mainframe. Simultaneously, the firm will be sending data out to the SPI team, some of which may be sensitive. Security devices, locking codes and passwords are all ways in which data can be protected, and portables, removed every day, can also help shield information. However, the real test is this: if anyone is that determined to break into a computer system and steal data, they will probably find a way to do it and the firm should not be forming partnerships with such people.

Expressing SPI team objectives

The objectives of a particular project may fall into any one of a number of areas. If the purpose of the project is to develop and launch new products or services, the objectives may be expressed in terms of market share to be captured. If it is a new production process, the objectives may be set out in terms of unit costs or volume produced. In the case of a new production plant, they may be expressed in contribution or profit terms, or as total costs within the agreed budgets. In the majority of instances, the firm will want to have project objectives relating to some financial measure of success.

When considering what objectives to set, the team leader should first determine the overall objective. This must be done by reference to the two sponsoring executives. Out of this, it should be able to determine the situational objectives – those pertaining to a specific part of the work programme – as the scheduling of the work begins. However, an intermediate step should first be addressed, that of critical success factors.

Critical success factors (CSFs)

Having identified the overall objectives, managers can now turn their attention to the critical success factors – the most important subgoals of the work programme. Achieving consensus on CSFs is absolutely vital.

In one famous study by Heyvaert, the top 10 managers in 125 European firms were asked individually to identify their firm's most critical five objectives. In the study, the minimum number from each firm would be 5 and the maximum 50. The research team divided the 125 firms into three groups, the 40 most profitable, the 40 least profitable and the rest. Managers in the 40 most profitable agreed on a range of objectives between 6 and 12, while managers in the 40 least profitable suggested between 26 and 43. In other words, the managers of the 40 most profitable firms had a clear, and shared, sense of what they were trying to achieve, while the opposite was true of the least profitable. This link between clear, shared objectives was further strengthened when, as a consequence of the study, three firms in the worst category moved into the top category. Significantly, their top managers had spent time defining and communicating their objectives.

Setting CSFs is not easy, but it is made easier when managers are given the right tools for the job. A project charting model is shown on the following pages together with an explanation of how it works.

First, however, there are seven rules for setting CSFs:

1 CSFs should be dynamic, causing action. This is achieved by beginning CSF statements with the words 'We must...' or 'We need...'.
2 CSF's should follow the 'necessary and sufficient' rule. This means that team members agree that a CSF is necessary and that all the CSFs added together are sufficient to achieve the purpose of the project.
3 Each CSF must be devoted to a single issue. There must be no overlaps – the word 'and' is forbidden.
4 The CSFs should be a mix of strategic and tactical.
5 The maximum number of CSFs for any work programme is eight.
6 Each CSF should follow a 'verb + object' sequence.
7 Each part of the work programme should have an owner, but no owner should be given more than four parts to look after.

Charting the work programme

We need to find a way of charting the programme of work to be undertaken in a simple, visual manner that shows the priorities. A project chart (Figure 9.4) enables us to display the critical success factors and all the work programme components needed to accomplish the goals of the partnership.

The example given is from an SPI goal stated as: 'We want to achieve the highest, most consistent quality delivered anywhere in the industry.' The CSFs are ranged horizontally along the top, while the processes, listed vertically, are shown as P1 to P13. In completing the model, follow seven steps:

1 Place the firm's work programme in the left-hand column. The processes here include elements relating to the subject of attaining the highest product quality in the industry, the subject matter of the SPI. To get started, it does not matter in which order the processes are entered.
2 Along the horizontal line at the top of the page, enter the critical success factors. Again, the order is unimportant at this stage.
3 Next, focus on the first CSF on the left and ask this question: 'Which work programmes must be performed to superior standards if we are to achieve this CSF?' The object is to single out the few business processes that have a direct, primary impact. Many will have an impact on it, of course, but the team is looking for the essential ones. Work along the CSFs from left to right, asking the same question of each until all have been covered.

CRITICAL SUCCESS FACTORS

WORK PROGRAMME		Benchmark highest quality	Raw material quality	Supplier reliability	Internal cost comparison	Manufacturing practices	Count	Quality
Market research	P1	■		■		■	3	C
Measure satisfaction	P2	■					1	E
Monitor competitors	P3	■				■	2	B
Monitor complaints	P4		■				1	D
Research materials	P5	■	■		■		3	C
QA/QC procedures	P6		■		■		2	D
Manufacturing	P7	■				■	2	E
Find new suppliers	P8			■			1	B
Evaluate criteria	P9		■	■			2	B
Evaluate suppliers	P10	■		■			1	C
Evaluate systems	P11				■	■	2	A
Certify suppliers	P12		■	■			2	C
Set new standards	P13	■	■		■	■	4	C

Figure 9.4 Project chart

4 The list must then be subjected to the 'necessary and sufficient' rule. The team should ask itself two questions: 'Is each CSF really necessary for us to achieve our objective?' and 'If all these CSFs are achieved, will the team achieve its first objective?' If the team answers 'No', it must identify what else is needed. Any new work programmes must have an owner in the SPI team.

5 Total the number of CSFs for each work programme and enter that number in the 'Count' column. The most important work programmes are those with the highest number of CSF impacts.

6 The model has a five-point 'quality' scale from A to E. Here, the team must be completely honest in ranking the quality with which each business process is currently performed, not the quality which the team would like to see. The 'Quality' column can now be filled in. The result of completing the two right-hand columns will be a numeric/alpha rating for each part of the work programme.

7 The team can now visualize or shade boxes showing relative importance. The work programmes with the highest number of CSF impacts combined with the lowest letter (D or E) denote the areas to which the team must devote its greatest energy if it is to improve the

quality of the process recognized as having high criticality. Conversely, another area of the graph will have a cluster of boxes with a low number of CSF impacts where the existing quality of the process is felt to be high (A or B). These areas need the least attention for the team to achieve its objectives. In this example, the team would need to concentrate its early efforts against P13, P1 and P5.

Structuring and scheduling the programme

A useful tool in designing work programme phases is the Gantt chart, named after one of its originators, Taylor and Gantt. The technique dates back to the early part of the twentieth century, but is still useful in planning general tasks against time. A Gantt chart is shown in Figure 9.5, where the example used is building an extension to a manufacturing plant. Only some of the tasks necessary to complete the work are shown here.

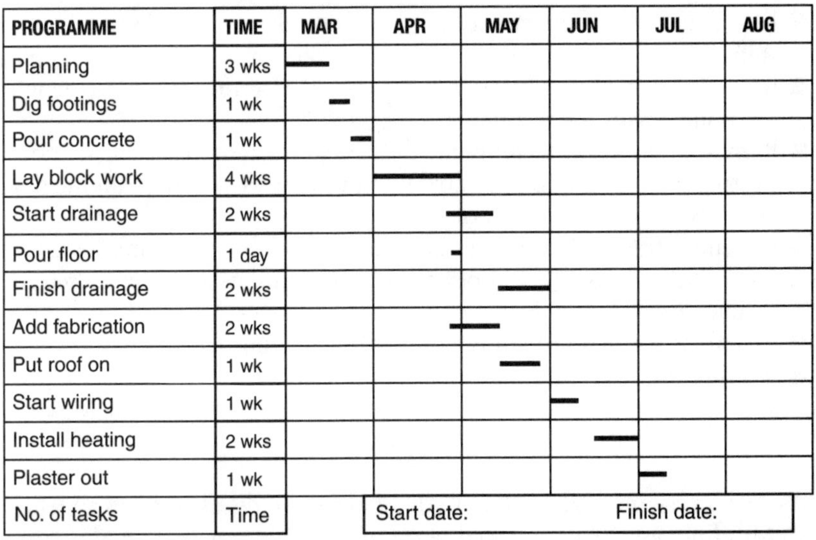

PROGRAMME	TIME	MAR	APR	MAY	JUN	JUL	AUG
Planning	3 wks	▬					
Dig footings	1 wk	▬					
Pour concrete	1 wk	▬					
Lay block work	4 wks		▬				
Start drainage	2 wks			▬			
Pour floor	1 day			▪			
Finish drainage	2 wks				▬		
Add fabrication	2 wks			▬			
Put roof on	1 wk				▬		
Start wiring	1 wk				▬		
Install heating	2 wks					▬	
Plaster out	1 wk					▬	
No. of tasks	Time	Start date: Finish date:					

Figure 9.5 Gantt chart

A Gantt chart has the advantage of enabling the team to see, on a single sheet of paper or screen, how the work programme can be scheduled, where work may be done in parallel with other tasks, and start and finish times for each part of the programme as well as for the whole. However, it is less useful as a control tool, not being sufficiently detailed or specific. For this we need another tool.

A more recent development in quantitative work programme management tools is the critical path method (CPM). This can be used to plan, schedule, analyse and control even the most complex of work programmes. CPM provides a means of determining:

■ Which tasks and activities of the many that must be completed are critical in their effect on total programme time, and therefore must be given the closest attention.
■ How best to schedule tasks and activities in order to meet target dates at minimum cost.
■ How work programme times and costs can be reduced or shortened in cases of potential overrun – a common problem.

Some other advantages of CPM include:

■ It can be used at every stage of a programme of work, from planning through analysis of alternatives, scheduling, budgeting and controlling tasks and activities comprising the partnership's work.
■ It can be applied to a wide variety of types of work.
■ It is a simple and direct way of visualizing the complex interrelationships of a work programme, even though these may be far from simple.
■ It is easily communicated by means of a graph, even to people unfamiliar with the technique.
■ It enables the team to pinpoint the tasks and activities that are critical to meeting deadlines, contributing to more accurate planning and better work and cost control.
■ It enables the team to study the effects of crash programmes – when a firm throws money and people at a programme in order to reduce its duration – if they become necessary.
■ It enables the team to study potential or real bottlenecks.
■ It leads the team to make reasonable estimates of total work programme costs for various completion dates, allowing them to select the optimum schedule.

As with every management tool, there are some disadvantages to using CPM; although these are listed here, they should not deter teams from adopting the technique. The many benefits of CPM outweigh its relatively slight weaknesses. The disadvantages are as follows:

■ CPM is difficult to apply to programmes where the collection of tasks and activities necessary to complete the project cannot be, or have not been, well defined. This should apply to only a small number of SPI tasks, and anyway, it is also true of other techniques. The real weakness is more likely to lie in team planning or poorly defined goals.
■ Problems exist where work programmes consist of tasks and activities that can be started and finished independently of one another. CPM works best when there is a continuous flow to the project.

■ Data calculations for large, complex projects can be tedious. However, to a great extent this can be overcome with the application of computer software programs designed to run on small PC systems.

Getting started on using the critical path method is relatively straight-forward. There are two methods, one computer based, the other manual. Apart from this distinction, however, they are the same. There are so many variations of computer programs that it is not possible to list or evaluate them here. Instead, we shall concentrate on the manual application of CPM, since an understanding and mastery of the manual process will give the SPI team a head start using a computer. Those already using a computer program may also be interested in knowing how the model works.

An example of a completed project graph, again using the same factory-building example, is shown in Figure 9.6. In this example, the critical path is a, b, c, d, j, k, l, n, t, s, x and is 34 days. If the contractor needed to finish this project in less time, it would need to find ways of shortening task time on this critical path. It is important to note that there can be more than one critical path for a given programme of work. In fact, it is another advantage of CPM that it has the ability to demonstrate this at an early stage, enabling the team to select the optimum one.

To construct a graph using CPM, follow the guidelines set out below.

1 Begin by dividing a sheet of A4 paper into four columns. Start in the extreme left-hand column by listing each task necessary to complete the programme of work. The team's first attempt should concentrate on getting the tasks down on paper. Now give each task a letter: a, b, c and so on, marking these in the second column. Lower case is normally used for this. Tasks should now be listed in order of their sequence.
2 Against each task, enter in the third column the predecessors of each task. For example, the predecessors of task c might be tasks a and e.
3 Next, in the fourth column, enter the estimated time required to complete each task. This is primarily a function of the team's experience, or that of someone else who may be consulted for expert knowledge. Any time denomination can be used: days, weeks, months, as long as it is used consistently. For most programmes, days will be the preferred denominator. Time is denominated by figures: 1, 2, 3 and so on.
4 Each task is now drawn on graph paper as shown in the figure, using a circle for each one. Its identifying task letter and time number are placed within the circle. A description of each task can be entered alongside each circle for ease of reference or can be shown separately as a key.

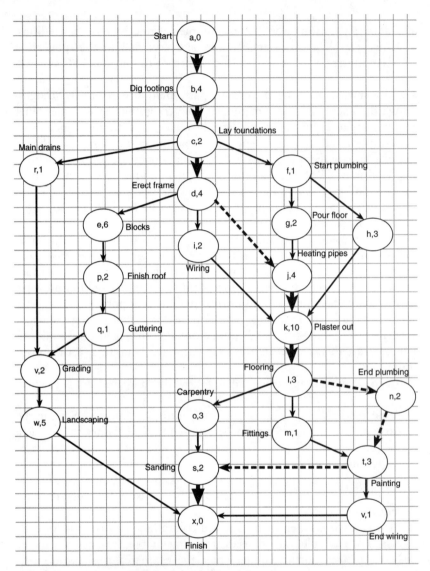

Figure 9.6 Critical path method

5 Circles can now be joined by lines indicating sequence relationships. Arrows on the lines indicate the task's immediate successors, with the arrows pointing to the successive task. All circles (tasks) with no predecessors are joined to the 'start' circle, and all circles with no successors are joined to the circle marked 'finish'. The start and finish circles represent tasks of zero time length.

6 The CPM graph now represents a number of different 'arrow paths' from start to finish. The time taken to traverse each path is the sum of the times depicted along that path. The critical path is the longest

path in time from start to finish. It shows the minimum time required to complete the entire project. In our example, 34 days is the minimum time needed.

The critical path can also be thought of as the bottleneck path. Only by finding ways to shorten jobs along the critical path can the overall project time be reduced. The time taken to perform non-critical tasks is irrelevant. The practice of crashing all tasks remaining in a work programme when overruns occur is therefore unnecessary, and a waste of effort, as CPM analysis will clearly show the tasks that are worth crashing if time is to be saved. Typically, this is no more than 10 per cent of all the tasks involved in completing the work. One further point of importance is that if a way is found to reduce overall time by shortening the critical path, the critical path may change so that tasks previously considered non-critical may now become critical.

If ways of shortening the critical path have to be sought, either tasks must be removed completely or the time taken to complete them must be reduced. Clearly, there is more than one way in which this can be accomplished. In the example given, the contractor might opt to put more carpenters on task d, assessing that this would reduce the time necessary to complete this task from four to two days. This would change the critical path slightly, causing it to pass through tasks f and g instead of d. The overall effect would be to reduce total project time by one day, even though two days had been shaved off task d. However, this might increase the cost of completing the programme and this would need to be examined as a part of the decision-making process.

There are four points to consider when seeking to shorten a critical path:

1 Changing one task has an effect on others and may change the critical path itself.
2 These changes frequently have an economic effect. In the above example, it may cost more to assign more carpenters to task d than is saved by completing the project a day sooner.
3 Physical issues have to be resolved when contemplating a change to the critical path. In the earlier example, it may not be physically possible to secure carpenters at the right time.
4 A delay in the start date will have consequences in pushing back the finish date. This needs stating, because too many work programmes seem to be managed on the basis that 'we can make the time up'. This is only true if ways of shortening the critical path can be found that are physically and economically feasible. For a more detailed analysis of critical path method, see Levy, Thompson and Wiest, 'The ABCs of critical path method', *Harvard Business Review*.

Using tools such as the project chart, Gantt chart and critical path method not only enables the team to plan, prioritize, schedule, monitor and control what is usually a highly complex set of activities, interwoven by the politics of working at the interface between two firms, it also allows the firm another opportunity to demonstrate its commitment and professionalism.

When things go wrong

As mice and men know all too well, even the most carefully laid plans can go wrong and, when they do, a procedure should be referred to that will allow a speedy resolution of the difficulty. We must be careful at once to delineate between technical problems, for which there is a problem-solving methodology in place, and relationship problems. It is problems between individuals and between partners which cause the greatest headaches, although they are relatively rare.

Relationship problems usually start with personal difficulties between two or more individuals. Sometimes, they simmer away without ever getting in the way of the work; at other times they erupt and then fade away. Occasionally, they get out of hand and it is these occasions that hold the biggest danger to the partnership, because opinion polarizes and people take sides.

There are three levels at which problems between the two partners may be resolved:

1 At the level of two or more individuals, one or more of whom are SPI team members. For example, a team member representing the firm is disliked by one of the customer or supplier representatives with whom contact is made on a regular basis. Knowledge of the problem surfaces when it filters back to the team leader. If possible, such matters should always be settled at team level, if necessary and as a last resort by replacing a team member. So at the first level, the vast majority of problems should be solved by individuals or within the team.

2 The second level arises when a relationship difficulty or difference of opinion which cannot be resolved at team level breaks into the partnership domain at a senior level. By this time, it is too late for the team leader to retrieve the situation alone and referral should be made to executive managers. Fortunately for the partnership, these managers now know one another a great deal better than if the same problem had arisen in a traditional buyer–seller relationship. And with a modicum of luck, they will sort it out with no lasting ill feeling on either side.

3 If it reaches level three, a contractual dispute, the partnership is almost certainly over. The subject of contracts in strategic partner-

ships will be dealt with in the next chapter. An example contract is also given in Chapter 3.

It is generally a good idea for the firm to raise this subject informally and in general terms, following the second partnership presentation and as the work programme is being planned. There will be numerous occasions during this period when the two executives concerned will need to discuss a range of matters and the right opportunity is sure to arise. The firm should not create obstacles where none exist, but may propose instead a course of action to be followed in the event of disputes. Whether this ever finds its way into writing is another matter, although it will in any case where a formal contract exists. In most partnerships an understanding is enough, and the best time to prepare the ground for this understanding is at the same time as all the other planning work is taking place.

We have now gone past a step in the strategic alliance map (Figure 9.7).

Implement plan, monitor, replan	SPI team agrees and schedules changes, monitors, replans	SPI team

Figure 9.7 The strategic partnership model excerpt

The two firms are following standard management practice in observing and assessing actual results, comparing them with what was expected, and replanning where necessary.

We can now move to the penultimate step in the modelling process (Figure 9.8).

Evaluate study and form proposal	Identify wealth creation and propose best practice with business simulations	Internal consultancy

Figure 9.8 The strategic partnership model excerpt

10 Evaluating strategic partnerships

In this chapter we will explore some of the hidden reasons for firms entering into partnerships with one another and how this can be connected to the partnership evaluation process. The methods of assessing partnerships, as well as the criteria against which measurement takes place, are extremely diverse, but we will examine some of the more common approaches as well as discussing the two classes into which assessment falls.

Hidden agendas

In just about every situation where two firms or two groups of people do business together, a hidden, covert agenda operates alongside the overt one. Partnerships are no different. There is nothing sinister about such processes, it is merely that there are bound to be some issues, even in the closest of partnerships, which one side does not want to disclose to the other. To pretend that a business partnership could ever be otherwise is not realistic.

Hidden agendas can contain any of the following items:

■ The supplier has something – a piece of knowledge, knowhow, a service – that the customer wants. A partnership is rarely entirely based on getting it, but it offers the perfect opportunity once the partnership has been entered into for other reasons.
■ The supplier wants to tell the customer something that is very difficult for any supplier to say to any important customer: a supplier's objection to constant demands for improved payment terms, for example. The issue is allowed to surface within the context of the SPI team instead and is fed back in that way. It is much less threatening to both parties.
■ The customer believes that volatility in the supply market makes the job of ensuring continuity of supply very difficult or unmanageable. This may be part of the reason that the customer engages in a partnership, but never discloses this to the supplier. The customer would then use the partnership to increase knowledge of the supply market.
■ The supplier is faced with a situation where several competing firms are all more or less the same. A partnership is one way to resolve this dilemma, gaining, as it does, the inside track. Few suppliers would explain their rationale to the customer.

■ Either partner cannot see clearly how some obstacle is to be overcome and recognizes that a certain partner may be able to provide something to fill the gap. The resulting partnership is authentically based on several other factors, but the hidden agenda still exists.

Variance analysis

The great majority of partnership differences are not between people but between planned and actual partnership performance. Some particular action was supposed to produce a specific outcome, but something else happened instead. A variance has occurred and a variance analysis is called for. Variance analysis is an accounting concept, originally related to the planned cost versus the actual cost of an activity when using standard costing. A cost is said to vary from the standard, either negatively or positively. Here, however, we will briefly examine the topic in its broader sense.

A variance can fall into one of four categories, each calling for a different response (Figure 10.1).

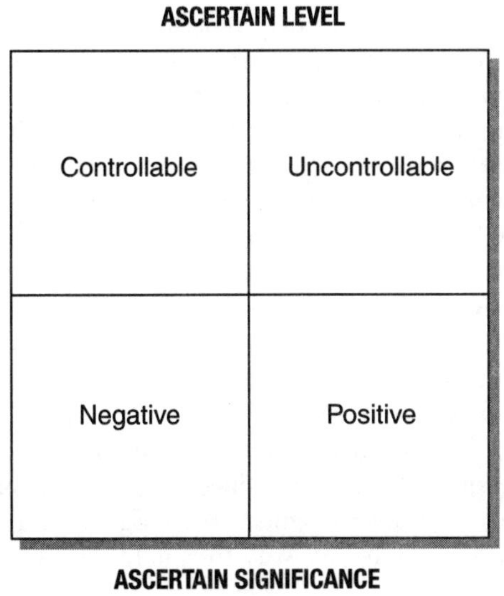

ASCERTAIN LEVEL

Controllable	Uncontrollable
Negative	Positive

ASCERTAIN SIGNIFICANCE

Figure 10.1 Variance analysis

Controllable and uncontrollable

Variances will fall into one of these two classes and it is important to determine which heading applies. Otherwise, time and money can be wasted in chasing the causes of variances that, in reality, lie beyond the control of anyone. The first check to be applied to a variance is the extent to which it is controllable or uncontrollable. This is far from being the black-and-white issue it appears to be, however, since it will depend on the organizational level at which control can be exerted. Top management can control some things simply because of their hierarchical level.

So the question must be: 'Can either or both of the partners control this issue and, if so, at what level?' Answering this question alone will not be sufficient to proceed, another question must be addressed first. This is: 'Will the cost of closing the gap be worth it?' In other words, how significant is the variance?

Positive and negative

It is easy to dismiss positive variances on the basis of their being good news. It is as though the focus should always be on the bad news – the adverse variances. Examining positive variances can be very rewarding, however. It often illuminates how something was achieved, making it easier to replicate. Variance analysis, when it is concentrated on the positive and negative aspects, is in practice a search for what is significant. This means ignoring insignificance – a subjective judgement to some extent – and focusing on the material differences.

Gap analysis and brainstorming are both applicable to variance analysis, but again, significance must be the determining factor when deciding what to analyse and what action to take as a result. One issue is crucial, whichever method is used, and that is that the variables making up the situation in which the variance occurred must only be changed one at a time. If two or more variables are altered together, producing a better or worse result next time, the team will only know that there has been an improvement or a worsening of the situation, not what caused it. If something has changed since the previous analysis, it is quite possible that this may be the cause. Homing in on recent changes is sometimes a quick and effective way to isolate the causes of variances.

Qualitative partnership evaluation

In beginning this part, several observations should be made. First, both partners will make assessments of the partnership independently, and sometimes privately, and this will take place irrespective of any common evaluations agreed. The reason is sometimes due to the existence of a hidden agenda, but will mainly be because the partners will place different emphases on different aspects of the results and these may change over time. Secondly, the firm should strive to create, as part of the partnership way of working together, an evaluation model that becomes the public part of the process and that both firms use. This will help ensure that at least part of the total evaluation is made on common ground. One of the causes of difficulties in partnerships is that success and failure, those relative terms, mean different things to different people. The same success or failure, when viewed from one particular perspective, can be seen to have produced a result quite unlike that seen from the perspective of the other. And thirdly, both independent evaluations, as well as the joint one, are likely to attempt to fulfil the needs of objective and subjective judgements. All of these issues will be addressed in this chapter.

The two classes into which partnership, and most other business evaluations, fall are qualitative and quantitative assessment. We will discuss these in this order and can begin our discussion by examining an initiative that the firm should introduce at an early stage, ideally in the first three months of the partnership going live. The firm proposes working together to create a joint assessment model and, assuming that this is agreed, the work is then undertaken by the SPI team. Alternatively, they commission the study to be completed by others. The steps are agreed with the partner one at a time until an agreed format has been produced, or the people carrying out the work produce a format and present it to both parties for agreement.

The starting point in the process is to develop a common understanding of what performance standards are to be achieved. This is vital, because words, phrases and even numbers can have widely different interpretations. Once these standards have been agreed, the work programme can be evaluated according to a shared view of work performance and results.

The process can begin with the SPI team leader or with the sponsoring executive at steering group level. The overriding need is to establish views and opinions and, to do this, questions must be asked and answered. A structured methodology is best for this and the following model is offered as an example of how this can be done. It is presented as a series of questions that are addressed by groups within both firms, and compared and filtered until a form of words is determined by common consent:

Question 1 – What words do you associate with successful performance? How would you express this?

Question 2 – What do you understand by superior performance? What examples can you recall of giving or receiving superior performance?

These first two questions are important, not only in establishing agreement of what the words mean, but also because superior performance should always be the goal. The Japanese have a massive commitment to superior performance, usually referred to as 'quality'. It is universally known and it has paid off. Some of its results include:

- Huge advances in export markets.
- International recognition as a producer of superior quality products in such areas as motor cars, cameras, electronics and many others.
- Few defects. In Japan, defects are measured in parts per million, while the rest of the world still calculates in hundredths, expressed as a percentage.
- Exportation of knowhow, which the Japanese had originally imported from the USA then further developed themselves.
- Complete implementation of superior performance, almost as a national mantra. In other words, all employees are involved in it, including top management.
- Simple methods and techniques are used that everyone can understand. People learn from their errors and correct them. The follow-up – the performance improvement programme – is continuous and ceaseless.

Question 3 – What are the different factors that affect your definitions of superior performance?

Words mean different things to the same person at different times, depending on the situation and that person's needs and moods. When more than one person is involved, agreement becomes much more difficult. This is because of several factors:

- The same product or service can satisfy a different range of people's needs at the same time.
- People have and apply different standards.
- The performance we demand from others varies according to who those other people are.
- The performance standards we demand from others may not be the same as those we demand from ourselves.
- Our expectations are different. Among other things, they are shaped by past experience and what we know about a firm and its products.

Question 4 – Think of situations when superior performance was received from an individual or firm. What situations can be recalled when substandard performance was given? What tilted the judgement that it was substandard? When superior performance was received, what factors made the decision that

it was superior?

(The supplying firm should answer the same questions from the position of a provider.)

Our expectations, whether we have any written specifications and the judgement criteria used will be key determinants in deciding whether what was received or given was good or bad. Even though most people will have a degree of difficulty when it comes to describing these matters, we are rarely in doubt when we experience 'good' or 'bad' performance. Most people recognize both, but framing the words is crucial in a partnership setting.

Performance falls into three categories: personal; for the firm as a whole; and for its products and services. Consistently high personal standards of performance are essential for the overall impression of superior performance to be achieved. It is almost unimaginable that a firm or its products and services can consistently meet the demands of customers unless there are high personal standards being applied throughout the firm and to every part of the supply process.

Someone has to lead, to set challenging standards for others to strive towards, and of course this is the job of top management. However, the strategic alliance setting allows another opportunity to be developed. The SPI team can become a 'centre of excellence', setting the standards for others to follow. Once the standards have been set, they must be communicated to everyone in the firm. From there, they can spread through the partnership in a ripple effect. Each person's personal performance affects the overall performance of the firm. It is a two-way street. And it does not end there: the products and services produced by the firm reflect the standards of the people who work there.

Question 5 – How would you rate performance on these tasks?

A list of tasks should be specified which ask people to evaluate current performance levels in a variety of different situations. The evaluation can be proposed in a written form in which the tasks are listed and people are asked to rate them according to an agreed mechanism. Current performance evaluations can be made in this way, looking at both firms. This is a helpful mechanism in establishing gaps, on both sides, between expectations and current reality.

Question 6 – How would you describe an ideal level of performance for each of these tasks?

This is an attempt to find words and phrases that bring the partners as close to recognizing their ideal performance levels as possible. It is only when the current level of performance is close to the ideal level that the partners will be satisfied, since they will be close to complying with their own expectations and demands. Answering Questions 5 and 6 also provides many clues in framing the objectives and targets that the partners should set for themselves.

Once the answers to all these questions have been analysed and interpreted, the partners have a code with which to evaluate, along one dimension at least, the work taking place inside the partnership. That dimension is qualitative and subjective. In addition to this, the SPI team should mount a series of formal presentations, one of which should be a biannual or annual audit.

Regular presentations form part of the work of an SPI team. 'Regular' means 'as often as necessary to achieve the objectives'. The twin objectives here are to portray a sense of professionalism, of 'being on top of the job', while simultaneously giving feedback on work programme tasks that have been completed, pointing the way to what comes next and enlisting support for future action as necessary. These presentations should be made to functional groups within both partner firms independently and, where convenient, to both together.

For example, the team may have been engaged in working in three customer departments, finance, systems and manufacturing, and two of the firm's own departments, finance and research and development. The tasks making up the work programme in each case will be specified, coded into the programme and implemented. Results must be communicated regularly to the groups of people concerned.

The best way to do this is by means of a formal presentation. Arrange it for the lunch break in a corner of the factory canteen, convenient meeting room or even factory floor. Depending on the content, it should last for between 15 and 30 minutes, but not longer. It should be a crisp, punchy explanation of the results achieved to date, the status of tasks not yet completed, the immediate future work programme, particularly as it affects those in the meeting, and requests for help where appropriate. There can be a question and answer session at the end.

People are invited to bring along something to eat or, if appropriate, sandwiches and refreshments can be provided. People from other functions having an interest in the work can be invited through an 'open door' policy. Briefings can be communicated directly to those who are directly affected by the work and by noticeboard bulletins to everyone else. Sponsoring executives on both sides should make a point of attending several briefings each year.

It will be possible in some cases to hold these briefings by combining functional groups from both firms, and this should be done wherever possible. It is another set of links in the policy of strengthening bonds between the two firms.

SPI team audit

The SPI team audit takes place either once or twice a year and is conducted jointly by the sponsoring executives. Its principal aim is to verify the extent to which the SPI team and the team leader grasp and are in control of the work programme to which they and other partnership resources have been allocated. The SPI team represents a significant asset to the partnership and the firm will have invested a great deal of time, money and energy into creating and developing it. The audit is the team's chance to demonstrate the effectiveness and standard of its performance, and top management's opportunity to make an assessment of the outputs versus the inputs.

The sponsoring executives should set up the audit by giving the team a month in which to prepare it. A full day or half a day should be allowed for the audit, depending on the volume of work to be covered as well as whether it is a biannual or annual affair. All team members should be present, though not necessarily for the whole day. The audit consists of a formal presentation, or perhaps to be more accurate a series of presentations, to the sponsoring executives. Other members of top management on both sides may attend as well, though once more not necessarily for the whole day.

Each topic presented will contain factual, quantitative data as well as subjective, interpretive opinion. It is the job of the sponsoring executives to assess the quality of all the material presented. Perhaps the first consideration is that the team leader must be able to demonstrate the ability to marshal the other team members to gather, organize, analyse, interpret and present material to colleagues. In this sense, the audit represents a real challenge to the team. It is a stiff test of many of the skills needed in team leadership, team involvement and management more generally. The abilities to clarify objectives, schedule a work programme, organize people over whom there is often no direct line authority, gather material from a wide variety of sources, interpret data correctly, make plans, implement action, pay careful attention to detail while seeing the bigger picture, give persuasive presentations which commit others to act and achieve meaningful results are all essential for managerial and business success.

The specific list of topics on which the SPI team will present will vary, not only between teams but also for the same partnership year on year. For example, if the partner has taken over a competitor during the past few months and this has affected the partnership in some way, executives may well want to hear how. In a more general sense, what problems have been solved and with what benefits accruing to the partners? How have the dynamics of working together changed? What are the expectations, goals and plans for the next phase of work? There would, of course, be many other items of interest, and the topics discussed below can therefore be used only as a general guide for setting up an account team audit.

Financial results

- What have been the key financial results?
- How do these differ from what was planned?
- What have been the main drivers and factors behind the financial performance?
- What has been the level of profitability on both sides?
- How has this differed from plan?
- What are the underlying reasons?
- What plans does the team have for getting any negative variances back on track?
- Has partnership profitability grown in line with the partners' own overall profit growth? If it is different, why?
- Have the underlying assumptions on which the objectives and strategies of the work programme based changed materially? If so, how?
- What have the partners learned that can be applied to profit planning in the future?

This component of the briefing should be given by the team leader or a designated team member with financial understanding.

Work programme

- How has the planned schedule of work actually occurred?
- What have been the significant factors in superior partnership performance?
- What steps have been taken, or are planned, to incorporate learning into work practices?

Products and services

- What are the implications for products and services of any of the changes explained above?
- What is the status of any new process, product or service development ideas currently in the pipeline?

Expectations

- Have expectations been met on both sides?
- How satisfied are both partners with what has taken place?
- Where does greater energy need to be focused?

Personalities

- How well have people worked together?
- How does the team rate the strength of the various functional relationships?
- Are there any problems that need to be addressed?

Future

- How does what has happened so far in the life of the partnership force a rethink in terms of what is possible in the future?
- Does this represent a significant departure from the original plan?
- What are the implications of this?

With variations according to circumstances and taste, these are the main planks of the SPI team audit. Both partners will form opinions and make evaluations based on what they see and hear. In most cases these will be shared with one another, either immediately following the audit or at a suitable time afterwards. Something may be seen in the audit that causes one or both partners to ask for more information or clarification, or both will be entirely satisfied with the outcome of the audit. Either way, the partners will be in a much stronger position when it comes to judging the inputs and outputs of each team, even though much of the evaluation to date has been qualitative.

Quantitative partnership evaluation

We should begin by establishing a simple fact: profits come from customers. We talk of 'value added' when referring to the manufacturing or distributive process, and it is common practice in many firms to 'transfer price' products and services between divisions, some even making a 'profit' in the process. We should really be speaking of 'cost added', because this is all that happens until an external customer exchanges money for goods and services. The simple truth is that there is only one place where value is added and that is at the interface between supplier and external, money-paying customer. And it is on this value that we must concentrate.

Over a given time period, say a month, the firm incurs costs and gains revenue from the goods or services it sells, including those sold within a partnership. These income and expenditure tables are totalled and compared to show the amount of profit or loss for that month. The picture becomes only slightly more confusing at the end of the accounting year when any profit is distributed among those who have a call on it. This will usually include Inland Revenue (tax), Customs and Excise (VAT), shareholders and the firm's own reserves. The accounting practices that become necessary at this point will show different levels of profit, with 'retained earnings' or 'profit for reserves' being the most accurate measure of what is left after everyone has been paid.

The concept of partnership profitability is a micro version of the firm's internal accounting procedures, and one that makes it possible to see the profit or loss arising from trading with one particular customer over a defined period. In reality, 'profit' is the wrong word here because it is really a 'contribution to profit'. This is because there are many costs, usually fixed or non-attributable, which have yet to be paid for.

Partnership profitability first identifies, then measures, each significant cost incurred in getting the programme of work completed. Partnership profitability systems can be either manual or PC driven. There are a number of software applications available for the PC, and this method tends to allow managers to focus on the interpretation, rather than the creation, of data.

Implementing a partnership profitability system (PPS) takes management willpower, commitment, time and money. Once the firm has made the decision to go ahead, it will be faced with two alternatives: to build a system from scratch or to buy someone else's. The decision will often be determined by the needs and circumstances of each firm, but as a generalization it is often easier to buy such systems off the shelf in the knowledge that the bugs have been ironed out by someone else. In any case, building from scratch can be a laborious business, end-users often changing their requirements in mid-stream.

Before addressing this issue, however, two even more fundamental questions must be answered:

1 Why does the partnership need PPS?
2 Can it be supported over the long term?

By itself, PPS will not solve problems of poor performance: it will just point the firm in the right direction in terms of where to look for the questions and answers. If there is the slightest doubt that PPS is just another 'flavour of the month' and will be forgotten within a year, or that it might not be affordable in a year, then the firm should abandon any notion of investing in such a system now. Supporting a PPS system will depend on both the need and the resources available within the firm.

Every solution must be tailored, but some general principles should help in determining the extent to which a partnership would be well served by a PPS system:

■ Does the firm plan one partnership or several? If only one, the resources necessary to set up a PPS system might not be worth the effort. In this case, some other method must be found to determine the additional costs and contributions arising from the partnership.

■ Is the cost or contribution item significant? Each firm must decide what 'significant' means to it. Insignificant costs or revenues generally do not need a PPS system approach.

■ Can the data be collected easily? There is a cost in any form of data collection, but the general rule is that if it costs more to collect the data than its value once obtained, it is probably too costly. Often, the difficulty with this question lies in knowing the future value of data. More often than not, this has to be an estimate. Remember that costs have a habit of occurring before they are supposed to and are greater than was forecast, while revenues and profits arise later than planned and are lower.

■ Will the results be understood by the user? It is clearly important that PPS systems are user driven and user friendly. They can be either paper or software based but, either way, it is vital for account team negotiators to have a significant input at the design or remodelling stage. Some training in understanding the fundamental principles of finance might be in order.

■ Can the user directly and positively influence actions based on the results of the PPS reports and analyses? If not, there is little point in having the information. It might be nice to have graphs and printouts, but if they cannot be used directly to influence the course of partnership programming, there is little point.

■ Can changes in performance be measured and consequent action taken? This will relate to the quality of the data produced by the PPS, the quality of thinking and decision making within both firms and their flexibility in responding to a wide variety of situations.

Assuming that the firm has made the decision to go ahead with a PPS system, and has recognized that what it will get is essentially a empty shell that will need filling before it can be used, it is ready to move to the next step. It must now determine how a plethora of costs are to be apportioned when setting up the system. This is usually more of a problem when considering indirect costs in general and some types of financing cost in particular. There are many choices to be made, not least between the various costing approaches the firm may use. For example, which costs, including overheads, are to be allocated to the partnership and on what basis? Following the advice of the finance executive is normally the best option. Once a system for allocating cost has been worked out, it can be applied to any future partnership as well, with exceptions being made as appropriate.

Assuming that the firm has decided to invest resource in a PPS system, but has not yet decided how to set it up, managers will be faced with resolving several issues of principle. During the development or commissioning phase these will become logistical matters, but for the moment the firm must consider the key building blocks of a PPS and their implications across different business functions.

Five overarching principles should guide the development and application of a PPS. They are:

1 Costs need to be significant. It is a waste of time, money and other resources to capture insignificant costs. It is only the significant costs that are likely to make any material difference either way.
2 Costs must be captured and delivered on a timescale that matches their usage. If the work programme relates to a business cycle based on 13 four-week periods, capturing data on a calendar-month basis because this suits internal accounting procedures will cause more problems than it resolves.
3 Costs must be captured efficiently, including cost efficiently. To repeat an earlier point, there is no point in spending more time or money capturing the data than the data is worth. Additionally, the contribution required from several departments, but particularly management accounting in gathering, sifting and processing the raw data, will be considerable. This input needs to be planned if the most efficient use is to be made of this valuable resource.
4 PPS data must be easily and simply communicated to the team leader and others who are supposed to act on it. 'User friendly' should be the watchword of all management reporting and PPS is the same. Continuous printouts a foot thick will never get used properly because they are too daunting to look at and too boring to read.
5 The people to whom these data are reported should be able to influence them. Lots of things in life are interesting, but managers are paid to influence events to the firm's benefit. It follows from this that the construction of data for presentation and action purposes should focus on showing data which managers can use to do just that.

As mentioned above, the resource requirement from the firm's own management accounting function, especially if the system is to be built from scratch, will be considerable. This is particularly true of the early phases of the project when a great deal of raw data must be harvested and input into the system. This has a cost, which should be considered a partnership cost.

There are many types of cost that can arise in a partnership. For any PPS system to work properly, it is necessary to identify them. In the majority of cases, the numerous and diverse costs associated with doing business in a partnership can be allocated to one of seven cost types:

1 *Trading discounts given by the supplier to the customer*. These include off-invoice discounts and can normally be categorized under the headings of long-term and repetitive. Examples include prompt payment discounts and step-volume discounts.
2 *Production costs*. These are the total product costs, including all product-related direct costs and attributable overheads.
3 *Overriders or long-term rebates*. These are performance-related costs linked to the customer's turnover and are generally paid after the event.
4 *One-time costs*. For example, tailor-made promotions, coupons, promotional payments, inventory writeoffs or special payments of one kind or another.
5 *Distribution costs*. The cost of handling, storing and transporting products or services through the supply chain from one firm to the other.
6 *Financing costs*. The internal cost of financing the business with a particular partner. This will mainly be the cost of credit and any specific settlement discounts, although in some cases it will include the cost of financing capital. Financing capital can be provided under the terms of a contract, either by the supplying firm or by a third party.
7 *Selling and support costs*. These will include the cost of the SPI team, including the team leader and any other executive overheads, plus items like order capture and processing.

Once these costs have been isolated and apportioned, a not insignificant task, decisions may be taken. PPS will accurately assess how a partnership performs in net contribution or net profit terms, and will enable partnerships to be compared to one another. Additionally, the impact of potential cost savings can be properly evaluated.

Any PPS profitability statement must show the seven levels of cost referred to above (see Table 10.1). Each cost category represents a different activity, enabling the team to focus on a particular activity with a better probability of success. For example, the 'Gross account contribution before overriders' line can be used to decide product mix decisions. Alternatively, elements of the 'Selling and support costs' line may be analysed when considering manpower reviews, staff support costs or processing procedures costs. A simple, preferably one-page layout should be devised showing all the costs under their seven headings. Where the partner is a supplier, this will be all that is necessary, but in the case of the partner being a customer, the revenues arising from the partnership will also appear.

The report document should be generated monthly or periodically and circulated to those who need the data and who are able to act on it. This must include sponsoring executives in both firms, as well as the team leader and any other permanent team members. There should be

Table 10.1 Example partnership profitability statement

	£	£
Gross sales value this month		450 500
Cumulative sales value this year		1 355 000
LESS:		
Trading discounts this month	78 000	
Cumulative trading discounts	112 000	
Net sales value this month (NSV)		372 000
Cumulative NSV		1 243 000
LESS:		
Production costs this month	160 000	
Cumulative production costs	440 000	
Gross account contribution before		
overrider this month (GACBO)		212 000
Cumulative GACBO		803 000
LESS:		
Overrider this month	9 000	
Cumulative overrider	24 000	
Gross account contribution after		
overrider this month (GACAO)		203 000
Cumulative GACAO		779 000
LESS:		
One-time costs this month (OTC)	78 000	
Cumulative OTC	200 000	
Account contribution after		
one-time costs this month (ACAOTC)		125 000
Cumulative ACAOTC		579 000
LESS:		
Distribution costs this month (DC)	88 000	
Cumulative DC	260 000	
Account contribution this month (AC)		37 000
Cumulative AC		319 000
LESS:		
Financing costs this month (FC)	14 000	
Cumulative FC	39 000	
Account contribution after financing		
costs this month (ACAFC)		23 000
Cumulative ACAFC		280 000
LESS:		
Selling and support costs this month (SSC)	12 000	
Cumulative SSC	38 000	
Net account contribution this month (NAC)		11 000
Cumulative NAC		<u>242 000</u>

Adapted from a model proposed by IGD
Reproduced from Chris Steward, *Managing Major Accounts*

some discussion between the two sponsoring executives, but the detailed planning and replanning should be done at SPI team level.

Many of the benefits of a customer profitability approach will have already become obvious. However, we can summarize the main non-financial and financial benefits:

- Managed opportunities to improve a specific work process or product.
- An improved understanding, by everyone involved, of how costs behave and interact with sales volumes within a partnership.
- Controlled opportunities to improve the firm's overall level of profitability.
- An increased level of real professionalism, as well as reinforcing that image among partners.
- Effective cost control, where this can be influenced by the SPI team or other managers.
- More effective management of communications due to a common approach.
- The opportunity to increase sales volume more profitably.
- Facilitation of a better trading relationship because the data to measure performance is readily available.
- An increased understanding of how one another's business works, leading to more profit opportunities being recognized.
- Continuous analysis of the contributions or profits made from the partnership.

Using PPS data for decision making

A key benefit of a PPS is that it enables decision making to be pushed further down the organization. Partnership profitability data should be made available to all standing members of the SPI team; one of their prime functions as they meet other specialists within the partnership is to make clear the cost and contribution ramifications of certain initiatives, proposals and decisions. Having the latest software toys can be enjoyable, but a business usually has to be profitable before it can be fun. PPS systems should guide the team to investigate all significant partnership costs and match them against the profit opportunities they provide.

It is probable that most partnership customers enjoy an element of overservicing. This is partly because the supplier has allocated a specific team to the partnership and feels duty bound to listen and act when the team leader reports a partnership servicing need. The team leader is fighting for scarce resources within the firm and can hardly be blamed for fighting their corner and trying to shout the loudest.

Within every partnership, the SPI team leader should be encouraged to identify areas where the customer might be overserviced so that these may be explored with the partner. Such analyses can often lead to an agreement to reduce service levels in one area and build them up in another, at no extra cost. Equally, service-level requests from new partners must be seen in the light of any new costs that might have to be incurred to meet the request. Equal attention should be given to trying to establish the value that each customer derives from each service component so as to place it in its proper context.

One of the most important factors in a partnership is partnership profit or contribution planning. Team leaders should be continually reviewing different actions against the likely costs, profits and other implications that such actions may trigger off. One of the many aspects of managing a partnership is regularly to review, with the partner, what benefits accrue from the partnership. This evaluation will occasionally be made relative to competing propositions. Remember that we are dealing with the concept of 'total value', which includes tangible products and all their associated services. And value, as almost everyone knows, means different things to different people.

The most critical factor when addressing the complexities of profit or contribution planning on an individual partnership basis is that it should take place before the event, not after it. Partnership suppliers sometimes spend too much time in response mode trying to answer queries raised by their customers, which will add to their costs in one way or another, rather than initiating profit-building actions. It is the responsibility of sponsoring executives to make sure that team leaders make the proper analyses of the profit options facing the firm at any one time.

As has been mentioned already, both partners will conduct a private evaluation of the partnership, probably informally at first. After some months, however, a more rigorous assessment will be made. The firm should be doing the same. Partnership evaluations pay. The principal risks of not conducting them are that the firm will have invested heavily – perhaps tens of thousands of pounds – without having the means to identify the success or failure of the partnership against its original objectives. Added to this, major investment made in people will have been partially or largely wasted, because the firm will not have been able to incorporate any learning gained from working inside an alliance, about its systems or culture. Finally, the firm will be unable to answer even the most basic questions concerning the initiative.

The following 'top 20' checklist is intended as a guide:

1 Was the partnership investment a success? Would we do it again?
2 How are we judging success and failure?
3 What important lessons can be learned that may be applied to the next one?

4   Has the partnership gone according to plan?
5   What did we do that made it go according to plan?
6   Which parts of the partnership have not worked according to plan?
7   Do we fully understand the reasons for this?
8   What unforeseen obstacles or problems were encountered?
9   How well did we cope with them?
10 What would we want to avoid next time?
11 What would we most like to carry over to the next partnership?
12 How well did our monitoring and control systems and methods work?
13 To what extent were our own and our partner's objectives met?
14 How accurate were our original costings?
15 How accurate were our revised costings?
16 How well were the work programme tasks allocated among the team?
17 What can we learn about SPI team design and composition?
18 How effectively were the techniques and tools applied?
19 What can we learn about scheduling and controlling the work programme?
20 How well did we cope with any significant problems?

There are three ways in which a partnership appraisal can be carried out: by the team leader responsible for the programme, by the sponsoring executive concerned, or by an independent third party. This last option might be another senior manager within the firm or a consultant specializing in this field. They each have their advantages and disadvantages:

By the team leader

Advantages	Disadvantages
Knows the detail	Too close to the project
Knows the data	Is associated with its outcome
Knows the decision process	Is committed to its outcome
Knows the main problems	Cannot see 'the wood for the trees'

By the sponsoring executive

Advantages	Disadvantages
Can take a detached view	Does not know the detail
Has more seniority	Cannot be completely objective
Knows the key decisions	Is committed to the outcome

By an independent third party

Advantages	*Disadvantages*
Is completely independent	Has to get the detail
No outcome commitment	Takes longer
Can be completely objective	Can cost more
Can see 'the wood for the trees'	

In spite of the apparent advantages of the first two approaches, neither is recommended because the disadvantages heavily outweigh the benefits. However, the third approach contains one or more advantages which have potentially greater benefits than the disadvantages, the main one being complete independence and objectivity. If the firm is to make lasting gains in increased knowledge and skill, it should opt for an independent partnership appraisal.

Ten important partnership lessons

From many evaluations of previous partnerships come the following lessons:

Determine project costs accurately

This is obviously difficult when contemplating the first partnership because no cost experience exists, although this can be partly overcome by working with an external specialist. There is a tendency to be too optimistic when calculating future partnership costs. Worst-case scenarios in two industry studies showed them to understate the worst case by 25 per cent in each case. Sponsoring executives and team leaders need to adopt a more realistic approach to costs and income, particularly during the early planning stages. An old aphorism applies here: 'costs will occur before they were planned, and will be greater; revenues will arise later than planned, and will be smaller'.

Cost the partnership out in phases

The two most obvious phases are everything leading up to the second partnership presentation and everything that follows it. One way to overcome the underestimation tendency referred to above is to prepare a detailed cost estimate for the first phase and a less detailed estimate for subsequent phases. If this sounds like an excuse for not doing a detailed cost study at the start, it is not. Top management usually approves only a tiny portion of the total budget at the beginning, directing this money towards the more detailed cost study that will be one of the results of the technical and commercial study.

It is then possible to prepare revised estimates for each phase as the partnership progresses. Use the commonly understood budgeting process described in Chapter 4, this will guide managers through what can easily become a minefield. Zero-based budgeting is an ideal tool when planning partnerships, since there is little previous data from which to work.

Anticipate risks and take steps to minimize their impact

Another important aspect of proper planning is risk anticipation. Not all risks can be predicted, of course, but a careful and thoughtful analysis early on, together with a contingency for the main risks if they occur, will help smooth the project if turbulence is encountered.

Disturbances generally fall into one of two categories: either commercial or managerial. Commercial risks arise when a technology does not work as anticipated, for example when a new design fails, when costs spiral out of control or when the product-market changes in some significant way. Managerial factors sometimes come into play as a direct result of a commercial failure: something goes wrong and the finger of blame is pointed. More often, however, managerial disturbance occurs because of a sense of territorial threat. A person or a group feels threatened by what they perceive to be an encroachment into their domain. Negative energy is applied, rarely to the level of sabotage since this is too obvious, until the atmosphere becomes poisoned. What begins as a small sore, with regular scratching can become a serious infection. Managerial issues are often overlooked during planning, yet an attempt to predict possible troublespots and reduce their impact can pay handsome dividends.

Analyse 'opportunity windows' carefully

Another common tendency is to develop a time 'window' during which the work programme must be initiated. This is usually based on a project chart timetable, culminating in the best 'window of opportunity' for the end result of the work.

In partnerships that last for several months or even several years, it is wise to revisit these assumptions and check them against a freshly validated view of the opportunity from a new time perspective. This is a highly dynamic problem. First, perceptions of opportunities change over time, often over a short time. Everyone knows that the view changes as you move along the road. Secondly, unless the situation is checked with the partner, gaps can open. And thirdly, a volatile cocktail is created when assumptions about situations, which also change over time, remain untested. A common assumption is: 'we both know where we're going, so there is no need to keep refocusing our effort'. An almost permanent analytical effort, aimed at clarifying opportunities and their time windows, is required to keep the partnership on a single track.

Select only the best partners

In the case of the main partner, the customer or supplier, this hardly needs to be restated, but it applies equally to what we might term 'junior partners'. These are the firms external to the partnership which may provide it with goods or services from time to time.

Selecting the best does not mean the least expensive; they have often been proved to be the most expensive in the long run. Firms would do well to select only those agencies or contractors which consistently demonstrate a thorough working knowledge of its practices and needs. Agencies with which the firm has worked before in a similar vein will need no introduction. Those that are new should be able to demonstrate, through their 'pitch', an understanding of the partnership concept and its underlying principles. Those that challenge current thinking should be welcomed. They may have uncovered, via their almost perfect objectivity, a new and better idea or a new slant on an old idea. Near-perfect objectivity is short lived, however, because there is a tendency for people to lose objectivity over time as they become immersed in the day-to-day activities for which they were hired. This can be overcome to some extent by keeping one or more agencies at arm's length, thus avoiding total immersion and keeping a degree of objectivity.

Improve partnership management by training team leaders

The best functional managers do not necessarily make the best team leaders. Careful identification of tomorrow's team leaders today means that, once the firm has one partnership up and running, other candidates can receive 'on-the-job' training by enabling them to work with more experienced team leaders.

First time around, team leaders and members have to learn by doing. The factor making this more difficult than usual is that learning is taking place in an environment shared by the customer, who is looking at everything under a microscope. Guidance can be obtained by hiring an external expert, with the emphasis on someone who has practical experience of the type of partnership envisaged. If this is to be the approach, the expert should be brought into the process as quickly as possible. Alternatively, the firm may seek a partnership team leader from among those experienced in managing a project team.

Either way, there is much to be gained from sending the candidates to a functional leadership programme. If the firm does not have the resources for this, many external training and development agencies exist which specialize in this field. This should be viewed as the beginning of a learning curve, not as an end in itself. Team leader and member candidates may need training in finance, physical distribution, computer software systems, or other issues specific to the planned programme.

Training requires attention just as careful as that given to any other facet of the partnership, though it seems to be overlooked the most frequently. Too many firms make the mistaken assumption that because someone has the title of 'leader', he or she automatically knows how to be one. There is so much riding on a partnership initiative that this can be a costly error. As soon as the first partnership initiative has completed a bedding-in period, typically about six months, the firm has one experienced team leader who can teach others. Managed properly, the partnership process becomes a learning experience for the firm as an entity. This means having a review process, reporting to the sponsoring executive, through whom the firm internalizes what it is learning, gradually building it into everyday work practice.

Do not bite off more than the firm can chew

This has particular relevance to identifying SPIs. Many SPIs seem attractive, but selecting one that the firm does not have the resources to see through will end in tears. Being realistic is not always easy, but it is vital to get the first partnership right or it will sour the entire concept for a long time.

A golden rule is to tackle only one partnership at a time. Do not even contemplate a second until lessons have been learned and absorbed and another set of resources put in place to get a further initiative off the ground. Consider several possible partnerships, selecting the one with the optimal risk–reward balance. Remember that resources are needed along a time continuum, not simply to start a partnership. If a programme of work is envisaged over nine months, resources must be budgeted for significant events in that period, with a contingency reserve.

Work only with authentic partners

Judgements in this respect must be made largely on past experiences of doing business with suppliers or customers appearing on the firm's short list, although the selection procedures given in this book should still be applied. Unfortunately, partnership has become a misused word in some commercial contexts; in a few cases, deliberately so. Unethical firms, or unethical individuals within a firm, have used the term and all its connotations to lure suppliers into an unequal business relationship. Such people and firms probably exist everywhere; usually their reputation precedes them, making them easier to avoid. Fortunately, inauthentic firms, in a partnership sense, normally form a small minority in any industry, the majority operating from an ethical base.

Put the measurement criteria in place

'Any road will take you there if you don't know where you're going,' as the Confucian maxim runs. It is vital that the subject of measurement is raised in early discussions with the intended partner, and certainly not later than the second partnership presentation. There will inevitably be problems if the two partners are measuring success against criteria that are opaque to the other partner. Financial measurement is a common tool, but even here, the partners must be careful to agree what figures will be used and in what way.

It is precisely because different interpretations can be placed on identical sets of words and numbers that a regular review process is built into the way of working. Different interpretations often arise because of the two firms' different goals and strategies and it is not going to be possible to change that fact. It is equally important that the partners feel confident enough to talk candidly to one another about the results, particularly when one party is disappointed. It takes time to develop this confidence, but the proper starting place is to design structured and regular reviews into the partnership from the outset.

Have an exit strategy

What will happen in the worst-case scenario – namely, that the partnership is not successful and one or both partners would like to end it – should be planned in advance. Very often, the prospective partner will open this topic for discussion at an early stage by asking the proposing firm what would happen if it were to enter into a partnership and then decided to leave it at a later date. So the issue must be faced, often publicly. In most cases, if it is agreed that the partnership should end, the ideal result would be to agree to continue working together, probably by reverting to the former supplier–customer arrangement. Proprietary knowledge gained during the partnership must be dealt with too, and it must be clear to whom this would belong if the partners decided to end the partnership. Usually, proprietary knowledge that is introduced by one partner is deemed to belong to that partner.

A greater difficulty arises when knowhow synergy has occurred, when knowledge has been shared and the result is greater than the sum of its previous parts. These matters can be addressed through the mechanic of a legal contract, or they can be a matter of goodwill; it depends largely on the nature and scope of the partnership and how well the partners know and trust one another.

The issue of partnership failure will be addressed in the next chapter, although the focus will be on the remaining step in the map of forging strategic partnerships: learning how to keep the alliance alive and thriving (Figure 10.2).

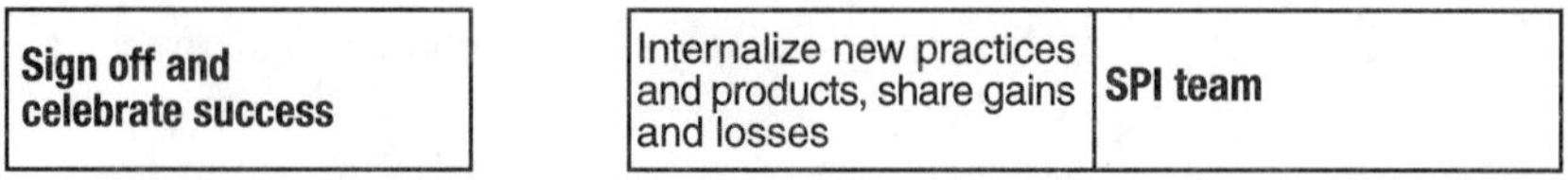

Sign off and celebrate success	Internalize new practices and products, share gains and losses	SPI team

Figure 10.2 The strategic partnership model excerpt

Sustaining strategic partnerships

In this final chapter we will explore the mechanisms that enable business alliances to prosper, as well as examining the major pitfalls that exist in commercial partnerships. We will also look at two examples of partnership failure to see what can be learned.

In practice, both positive and negative aspects relate mainly to the partnership criteria laid down in Chapter 3: trust, fairness, mutuality and wealth creation. These components are not hierarchical; they overlap one another across the entire landscape of an alliance. The proposal 'trust us' is rarely accepted at first: it takes time and involves a step-by-step approach. Trust is fragile and can easily be broken, often taking much longer to repair than to construct in the first place.

What, then, are the building blocks on which trust can be built and reinforced over time? To attempt to answer this we must see trust in both a moral and technical sense. The first two points of the five below deal with the moral dimension:

- *Never break a promise*. Broken promises are the single biggest cause of loss of trust and goodwill in business alliances. It usually happens by accident rather than design, but the result is the same. The best way for the firm to insure against this type of loss is only to make promises that it sincerely believes it can keep, even if this sometimes means offering the customer less than is desired. The golden rule is: 'aim to underpromise and overdeliver'.
- *Display integrity*. Saying is one thing, doing another. It is by our actions that others generally judge us, and this is equally true in a business alliance. In reality, partnerships formed on any other basis are doomed to failure. The early days and weeks are particularly critical, because the receiving partner watches every move closely. This is not in the hope of catching someone out, but is merely a statement reflecting human nature. The firm must work out the sensitivity points in advance of each initiative and work hard to display integrity at each one. Telling lies, even minor ones, and obfuscating unpleasant truths unearthed during the work programme are not the means by which integrity is displayed.
- *Stick to the script*. Once an SPI has been planned, keep to the work plan as closely as possible and only deviate from it after thorough consultation with the alliance partner. Moving away from the plan will produce unexpected results; even though many of these will be positive, one or two negatives will outweigh them in the customer's

mind. Particularly avoid introducing entirely new elements to the work programme without prior discussion and agreement.

■ *Work for the customer.* The firm's best interests lie in customers performing well and then reaping the appropriate partnership benefits. In part, this is the rationale for starting a partnership in the first place. The old maxim of 'never forget who pays your wages' no longer applies. It is the fruits of the partnership that 'pays the wages' of everyone concerned.

■ *Hold the big picture.* It is easy to get bogged down in the minutiae of an SPI once it gets under way, and equally easy to get side-tracked into blind canyons. Holding the big picture is simpler for the sponsoring executives on both sides and is a critical task for them.

Fairness and mutuality are connected. Decisions reached on the sharing of costs and profits, for example, must be thought of as being fair to both parties and recognizing that their respective contribution may vary from one initiative to another. The benefit of an extra point of profit, weighed against the overall risk of alienating the partner, will usually not be worth it over the long haul. When both partners recognize that, to some extent, their fortunes are bound together and that both are now taking decisions and implementing action from this standpoint, a critical moment has been reached.

Of course, nothing speaks like the numbers. The central purpose of creating an alliance is to achieve business outcomes considered difficult, unlikely or impossible when acting alone. These future realities, quite properly, will have quantifiable profit and loss account numbers added to them, and it is on these that attention will be focused – on both sides. If the numbers are not adding up, don't hide the fact. Having a partner means having more options and one of these is the application of mental power directed towards joint actions designed to get back on plan as quickly as possible. Trust and feelings of goodwill will be weakened by lack of consultation, and strengthened by openness and clarity of purpose.

Partnership pitfalls

Strategic alliances frequently proceed serenely from one phase to another and from one SPI to another. As with any other method of doing business, however, matters sometimes take a turn for the worse. Although not presented in any order of significance, among the most common causes of alliance difficulties are as follows:

■ *Unclear goals.* There are several possibilities here, all equally dangerous. First, confusion may arise if partnership goals are in conflict in some way with overall corporate aims. It may result from a conflict between the more specific partnership objectives of the partners. Third, the way in which goals are written may lead to management being pulled in several different directions at once, leading to confusion and inertia. The solution lies in agreeing common goals for the partnership, even if this means abandoning some earlier ones, while maintaining a clear recognition that some individual partnership goals are bound to be different. If corporate aims are too divergent, this can be sufficient reason to select another partner. Firms should not cut corners on agreeing goals and strategies to accomplish them; time spent early in the process can save heartache later on.

■ *Changes in management*. New managers are appointed who do not believe in this way of working. This is usually significant only when it occurs at a senior level. The only solutions are a renegotiation of the alliance, probably on different terms, or withdrawal.

■ *Lack of mutuality*. One partner perceives that the other is getting more out of the alliance or putting less in. This may be a perception only, or it may be the reality. The best approach is to address the issue openly, seeking to redefine the basis of mutuality.

■ *Lack of trust*. When this happens, it is most often in isolated pockets. For example, some of the members of one department or function do not trust the new partner or its motives. Working with these people and explaining the true purpose, motives and benefits is the most appropriate way to deal with this problem.

■ *Sensitive data availability*. Both partners must reveal data and information to the other on a general basis for the alliance to work at full effectiveness. Some of this information will be sensitive, and there will be a natural reluctance to release it. However, the speed at which this is asked for, as well as the depth of probing, are the two influencing factors. It is best to proceed slowly, gathering data and building trust simultaneously.

■ *One partner wants to end the alliance*. There may be many reasons for this, but the most likely causes are to be found in the partnership not realizing the ambitions of the partner, or in those ambitions changing. In some cases, both partners are looking for an exit. Continuing in such a relationship will engender such severe strains that a permanent rupture is possible. Ending the partnership on amicable terms is the best way out.

■ *The people do not work*. While every care is taken to select the right people as team leader and team members, something in the chemistry between team members causes friction. It may not seem like a major obstacle to outside observers, but it can easily lead to information and trust haemorrhages, ultimately causing breakdown. Another variant of this is a personality clash. Two big egos do not fit into one partnership very well, and this can be true at the SPI team or sponsoring executive level. Once more, considering this should be a feature of the planning process.

■ *Unexpected outcomes.* These can be pleasant or unpleasant, but only the latter represents a potential pitfall. There is always a risk of unexpected and unpleasant outcomes in strategic partnerships, but once sufficient goodwill has been established they can normally be handled without too much difficulty. Most can be foreseen in the weeks or days leading up to its uncovering, enabling a gentle landing. The key is to avoid trying to hide unpleasant surprises. Instead, be open with the other partner.

■ *Sabotage.* Projects can be sabotaged by what is known as negative energy or by plain inertia. Both can be destructive forces. Although quite rare, it sometimes arises among people who feel they have something to lose when their firm forms an alliance. Middle management is the most common area for this. Try to identify potential 'losers' before starting the partnership, taking steps to reduce or eliminate their concerns if possible. If it is not possible to do this, the sabotage must be tackled head on when it happens.

■ *Resource unavailability.* This has many variants, but can be caused by poor planning or by changes, foreseen or not, in circumstances. The partners may want to undertake an activity but cannot find the resources. This is a very common management problem and the same solutions generally apply: shift the resources from elsewhere, find new resources, or postpone or rephase the work.

■ *Goals not met.* Again, a common reality for managers. Possible approaches include redefining the goals, examining the strategies or circumstances surrounding them, the application and weight of resources used, or the number, organization or calibre of people employed.

■ *Change of strategy.* Top management changes the direction of policy and one result is that the imperatives that brought the partners together in the first place no longer exist. If this is the case, a mutually satisfactory exit is the best solution.

Occasionally, one or more of these pitfalls causes a complete rupture in relations. Trust breaks down, leading to eventual partnership paralysis. Alternatively, nothing specific goes wrong, there is just a feeling on the part of one or both partners that the partnership is not working. Either scenario is possible.

We will now look at two examples of partnerships failing, examining how it happened, what was done and what can be learned for the future.

Computer systems

A major firm in the design and building of computer systems in the financial services sector designed a partnership with a leading UK merchant bank, its customer. The supplier had experience of several other partnerships, all of them successful. The merchant bank was a long-standing customer and the two enjoyed good relations up to middle management level. The SPI was based on finding new and profitable ways to repackage existing financial data.

Senior managers from the two firms met and, after several weeks of discussions, agreed the basis for a partnership. A contract was drawn up, including a very tight confidentiality clause, and was signed. This provided for a split of new profit streams (profits that would not have existed but for the initiative) on the basis of 70/30 in the supplier's favour in the first year, 60/40 in the second year and 50/50 in the third year. The 'year' would begin on a date to be agreed in the future. Costs were apportioned on the same split but, of course, began immediately.

The SPI team was formed and started to schedule the work programme, which began smoothly. Reviews took place at several levels, as planned, and at one of these, six months after start-up, the partners agreed to initiate two new product-development ideas. However, development was interrupted by the acquisition of the merchant bank by one of its overseas rivals, one of several similar acquisitions taking place in the industry. SPI work was temporarily halted until the supplier could meet the new senior managers.

After a delay of five months, the new owners suggested that work recommence, but on different profit-split terms from those previously agreed. Several weeks of negotiation followed, but no agreement could be reached. Reluctantly, the supplier proposed reverting to the former supplier–customer arrangement. The new owners asked for compensation and this was refused.

The supplier asked for payment for the 30 per cent share of costs that were to be borne by the customer. This too was refused. In a sullen mood, the partners let the initiative die and reverted to their former method of working.

What can be learned from this episode? Two issues emerge for consideration.

Since takeovers and mergers were taking place in the industry, some thought might have been given to what should be done if it were to affect this particular customer in this way. Similarly, likely predators might have been considered. This process might have helped in decision making concerning the entire initiative. Secondly, and assuming that the firm had done this aspect of risk planning and had decided to go ahead with its eyes wide open, it would have been guided to a deeper consideration of its exit strategy. This might not have altered the partnership outcome, but it would probably have meant that future post-partnership business could be conducted on a more secure basis.

Glass manufacturer

A glass bottle and flask manufacturer had entered into several partnerships over a five-year period and so was experienced in developing this way of working. The majority of its alliances were with customers, but two were with suppliers. The firm now decided to develop a three-link partnership involving one of its key suppliers, a design agency, and one of its principal customers, a perfume house. The SPI was to find ways of incorporating new designs into manufacture and physical distribution more quickly, while simultaneously lowering costs. A second activity stream would examine the impact of design changes on production runs, a common problem being inventory management during changeover.

Discussions were held over a period of almost a year, the result of which was agreement between the three parties to begin. Six months was set as the time limit for the work, after which the three firms would review the situation to determine whether they wished to continue working together as real partners. An SPI team was formed from among staff representing the three firms, headed by someone from the bottle manufacturer.

The work was completed on time and in an atmosphere of growing cooperation. However, there were few clear recommendations and more unanswered questions than before. Several weeks later, the three firms agreed to act independently to implement several very specific points arising from the work, but not to continue with the partnership approach. Each expressed disappointment with this outcome but, despite harmonious working relationships, could not find sufficient commercial reasons to continue. They reverted to their former method of working.

What went wrong? The internal review conducted by the glass bottle manufacturer highlighted several possibilities. First, it may have taken on too much in trying to bring together the different goals and strategies of three firms, even though they were linked together in a macro chain. Despite their good working relationships, the team was being pulled in three directions and could not manage the conflicts this caused. Secondly, and related to this, the SPI objectives were insufficiently tight, which meant that team members tended to work to their own agendas rather than those of the SPI team, because the former were clearer. Finally, and again related to the first point, it seems probable that the lack of clear recommendations from the SPI team resulted from harmonious but fragmented working practices. With the benefit of 20/20 hindsight, a team leader with a more forceful personality might have helped.

These were two failures among several. There have been other failures, most occurring for reasons that can be identified and corrected. This really is the crucial point. The value of auditing partnership practices and outcomes, good and bad, perhaps with external assistance to begin with, cannot be stressed too highly. When mistakes are made, a structured problem-analysis approach will be of benefit. It may be through our mistakes that we learn, but we gain nothing from repeating the same ones.

The future

A question often asked is what will happen to the partnership once the SPI has been completed? The answer is that another will take its place. What is more, creating the second and subsequent initiatives will be considerably easier than creating the first one. There are many reasons for this, but the three most important are the following:

■ The two parties will have established a level of trust that enables smoother project transitions to take place between one piece of work and another. More and more will be possible with less time spent on permission seeking.
■ The partners will have learned to work with one another more closely, and this includes an understanding of the decision and other management mechanisms necessary for change to occur. This will speed the flow of work and the adoption and internalization of practices and outcomes.
■ Both members of the alliance will understand more fully the strategies employed by the other and will be able to recognize mutually beneficial opportunities that fit with existing policies. Improved opportunity recognition leads to the effective pursuit of bigger payoffs and fewer wasted chances.

The force of these three elements, when combined, is much greater than any of the individual components and becomes almost irresistible. As the realization grows that two separate business entities can work together to share costs, knowhow and profits, and the result can be better than either could achieve alone or by doing business together in the traditional way, an often unspoken commitment to continue is made. Managers on both sides actively participate together in searching for new opportunities to make additional profits. Ideas become initiatives. Plans are proposed. Acceptance has been achieved. A true strategic alliance exists.

Strategic alliances are not the only pathway to commercial success but, applied properly, partnerships of this nature are an extremely effective tool in helping management fulfil its strategic mandate.

References

Ansoff, Igor (1987) *Corporate Strategy*, Penguin Business, Harmondsworth, p. 43.

Buzan, Tony (1974) *Use Your Head*, BBC Publications, London, pp. 83–106.

Dobbins, R. and Pike, R.H. (1983) 'Capital budgeting techniques' in Fanning, D. (ed.) *Handbook of Management Accounting*, Gower, Aldershot, p. 68.

Ehrenberg, A.S.C., Hammond, K. and Goodhardt, G.J. (1991) *The After Effects of Consumer Promotions*, London Business School, London.

Heyvaert, Charles-Hubert (1988) 'Strategy and innovation in the firm', unpublished study, University of Leuven, Belgium.

Kotas, Richard (1989) *Management Accounting for Marketing and Business*, Hutchinson, London, pp. 112–14.

Levy, F.K., Thompson, G.L. and Wiest, J.D. (1963) 'The ABCs of critical path method', *Harvard Business Review*, September/October.

Moss Kanter, Rosabeth (1984) *The Change Masters*, Unwin, London, p. 134.

Steward, Chris (1996) *Managing Major Accounts*, McGraw-Hill, Maidenhead, p. 82.

Index